this book belongs to...

Southern Living

SCOOPED

Ice Cream Treats, Cheats, and Frozen Eats

Oxmoor House®

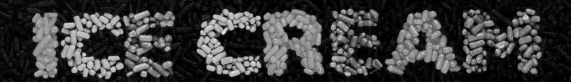

Mmmmm..........

Hot fudge, buttery cake, swirled ice cream, crushed cookies, whipped cream with a cherry on top . . . What could be more delicious? We've taken everything you love about dessert and spun it into one fantastic explosion of frosty sweetness—plus, it's even easier than you'd ever expect. By taking advantage of the vast selection of ice cream at the grocery store, making amazing and over-the-top ice-cream cakes, pies, sandwiches, shakes, and more is super-simple and crazy-fun!

Packed with over 100 sprinkled, drizzled, stacked, and dipped wonders, plus loads of from-scratch ice creams, toppings, syrups, cookies, and crusts, *Scooped* shows you how to make impressive and indulgent ice-cream desserts, without all the fuss. Learn how to throw a customized ice-cream social (page 6) or make a towering Red Velvet Ice Cream Cake (page 139). Cool down with a Key Lime Ice Cream Pie (page 90) or make some Mini Ice Cream Peanut Butter Cups (page 20) for your next get-together.

With brand-new twists, tried-and-true favorites, and frozen treats with a Southern spin, you'll find many new chilly sweets to try. We say, "Keep the brain freezes coming!"

Allison E. Cox

Allison E. Cox, Editor

HOST THE COOLEST PARTY ON THE BLOCK!

EASY ANYTIME PARTY
MEMORABLE MAKE-AHEAD BASH
SPECIAL WEEKEND CELEBRATION

EASY ANYTIME PARTY

Let the store do the work for you, and let your guests assemble their favorite, over-the-top sundaes.

WHAT TO BUY

- pints of various flavors of ice cream
- sugar cones and waffle cones
- cookies and wafers of all kinds
- ice-cream syrups and sauces
- sprinkles and colorful candies
- chopped nuts, candy bars, and cookies

MEMORABLE MAKE-AHEAD BASH

Make everything ahead of time, and freeze.
When your guests arrive, all you need to do is serve!
Use trays of ice to keep treats cold and keep
colorful napkins handy for serving.

MENU

Caramel-Almond-Vanilla Cones (page 42)
Dipped Ice Cream Whoopie Pies (page 26)
Mini Ice Cream Peanut Butter Cups (page 20)
Strawberry Cheesecake Ice Cream Cupcakes (page 124)

SPECIAL WEEKEND CELEBRATION

For a party that's sure to delight, throw out all the stops by making everything from scratch—a pretty cake, homemade ice cream, cookies, and toppings!

MENU

POPS, BONBONS, BARS, AND MINI TREATS

Piled up high in a bowl for a party, or enjoyed one at a time on a plate, these flavor bombs with a crunch are sure to become a favorite treat. Pour over the caramel just before serving.

CINNAMON-CHOCOLATE CHIP ICE CREAM BALLS

makes 6 servings   hands-on time 15 min.   total time 2 hours, 15 min.

1½ cups cinnamon-sugar whole wheat-and-rice cereal, crushed
½ cup semisweet chocolate mini-morsels
1 cup finely chopped pecans (optional)
½ gallon vanilla ice cream
½ cup jarred caramel syrup

1. Combine crushed cereal, morsels, and, if desired, pecans in a large bowl.

2. Scoop ice cream, and shape into 6 (3-inch) balls.

3. Roll balls in cereal mixture, coating evenly. Place in a 9-inch square pan; freeze 2 hours or until firm. Serve immediately, or store ice-cream balls in a zip-top plastic bag in the freezer. Drizzle with caramel syrup before serving.

note: We tested with General Mills Cinnamon Toast Crunch cereal.

the scoop · · · · · · ·

Give these versatile truffles your own spin by using different flavors of ice cream, like chocolate, cinnamon, or butter pecan.

17

BITES

These individual treats can stay in your freezer for when you need a late afternoon pick-me-up. For a party, just fill a tray with ice, and arrange these bonbons in candy wrappers over the ice.

COFFEE ICE CREAM BITES

makes 24 servings   hands-on time 25 min.
total time 2 hours, 25 min.

1½ cups coffee ice cream
Parchment paper
1   (7.25-oz.) bottle chocolate ice-
     cream shell topping

½   cup chocolate-coated coffee
     beans, crushed

1. Scoop ice cream into 1¼-inch balls using a small ice-cream or cookie scoop; place on a parchment paper-lined baking sheet. Freeze 1 hour.

2. Remove 4 ice-cream balls from freezer, and place on a wire rack in a jelly-roll pan. Shake ice-cream shell topping, and squeeze over ice-cream balls, coating top and sides completely. Immediately sprinkle with crushed coffee beans. Return to freezer. Repeat procedure with remaining ice-cream balls, shell topping, and crushed coffee beans. Freeze 1 hour or until firm. Serve immediately, or store ice-cream balls in a zip-top plastic bag in the freezer.

MINI ICE CREAM PEANUT BUTTER CUPS

makes 12 servings   hands-on time 15 min.
total time 1 hour, 13 min.

⅓ cup vanilla ice cream, softened
3 Tbsp. creamy peanut butter
Miniature paper baking cups
¼ cup chopped dry-roasted peanuts

1 (7.25-oz.) bottle chocolate ice-cream shell topping
Parchment paper

1. Stir together ice cream and peanut butter in a small bowl; freeze 10 minutes.

2. Place paper baking cups into 12 miniature muffin cups. Spoon ½ tsp. peanuts into each cup, and top with 1 tsp. shell topping. Freeze 5 minutes.

3. Quickly spoon ice-cream mixture into each cup; drizzle shell topping evenly over ice cream, coating completely. Immediately sprinkle remaining peanuts over shell topping; freeze 1 hour or until firm. Serve immediately, or layer between sheets of parchment paper or wax paper in an airtight container, and store in freezer up to 1 month.

ICE CREAM BOURBON BALLS

makes 34 balls   hands-on time 21 min.   total time 7 hours, 51 min.

2   cups vanilla ice cream, softened
½   cup toasted finely chopped pecans
3   Tbsp. bourbon or whiskey
30 vanilla wafers, finely crushed (about 1 cup)

Parchment paper
2   (8-oz.) packages semisweet chocolate baking squares, chopped

1. Stir together first 4 ingredients in a medium bowl. Freeze 6 hours or until firm.

2. Scoop ice-cream mixture into 34 (1¼-inch) balls using a small ice-cream or cookie scoop. Place on parchment paper-lined baking sheet. Freeze 1 hour.

3. Microwave 8 oz. chocolate in a medium-size microwave-safe bowl at HIGH 1 to 1½ minutes or until melted and smooth, stirring at 30-second intervals. Cool 5 minutes or until barely warm.

4. Remove 4 ice-cream balls from freezer. Quickly dip balls, 1 at a time, into melted chocolate using a fork and allowing excess chocolate to drip off. Immediately place on a parchment paper-lined baking sheet. Place in freezer. Repeat procedure with remaining melted chocolate, dipping 17 ice-cream balls.

5. Microwave remaining 8 oz. chocolate in a medium-size microwave-safe bowl at HIGH 1 to 1½ minutes or until melted and smooth, stirring at 30-second intervals. Cool 5 minutes or until barely warm. hRepeat dipping procedure, 4 balls at a time, with melted chocolate and remaining 17 ice-cream balls. Freeze 30 minutes or until firm. Serve immediately, or store ice-cream balls in a zip-top plastic bag in freezer.

the scoop • • • • • • •

To keep the melted chocolate from getting too cool for dipping, only melt half at a time. The key to success here is only removing about 4 ice-cream balls from the freezer at one time.

These bonbons are reminiscent of the classic Almond Joy candy bar, but they are so much more decadent with a filling of coconut-packed chocolate chip ice cream. Guests are sure to be impressed.

CHOCOLATE MACAROON BONBONS

makes 28 bonbons   hands-on time 27 min.
total time 6 hours, 20 min.

1 cup sweetened flaked coconut
2 cups chocolate chip ice cream, softened
½ tsp. almond extract
Parchment paper

3 (4-oz.) semisweet chocolate baking bars, chopped
¼ cup whole natural almonds, chopped

1. Preheat oven to 350°. Place coconut in a single layer in a shallow pan.

2. Bake at 350° for 7 to 8 minutes or until toasted, stirring occasionally. Remove from oven, and cool completely (about 15 minutes); reserve ¼ cup.

3. Combine ice cream, almond extract, and remaining ¾ cup toasted coconut in a bowl; stir well. Freeze 4 hours or until firm.

4. Scoop ice-cream mixture into 1-inch balls using a small ice-cream or cookie scoop; place on a parchment paper-lined baking sheet. Freeze 1 hour.

5. Microwave chopped chocolate in a small microwave-safe bowl at HIGH 1 to 1½ minutes or until melted and smooth, stirring at 30-second intervals. Cool 5 minutes or until barely warm to the touch.

6. Remove 4 ice-cream balls from freezer. Quickly dip balls, 1 at a time, into chocolate using a fork and allowing excess chocolate to drip off. Immediately place on a parchment paper-lined baking sheet, and sprinkle with almonds and reserved toasted coconut. Place in freezer. Repeat with remaining ice-cream balls, chocolate, almonds, and coconut. Freeze 30 minutes or until firm. Serve immediately, or store in a zip-top plastic bag in freezer.

These small cream puffs are surprisingly easy to make, but they have a fancy look that's perfect as a light dessert beside a cup of coffee when company comes for dinner.

PROFITEROLES WITH COFFEE ICE CREAM

makes 2 dozen puffs   hands-on time 20 min.   total time 1 hour

¾ cup all-purpose flour
1½ tsp. sugar
⅓ cup butter
3 large eggs, beaten

Parchment paper
1½ cups coffee ice cream
1 cup hot fudge topping

1. Preheat oven to 400°. Stir together flour and sugar.

2. Bring butter and ¾ cup water to a boil in a 3-qt. saucepan over medium-high heat, stirring occasionally. Immediately remove from heat, and quickly stir in flour mixture all at once. Beat with a wooden spoon until mixture is smooth and leaves sides of pan, forming a ball of dough. Gradually add eggs, beating until mixture is smooth and glossy.

3. Drop dough by rounded tablespoonfuls onto a parchment paper-lined baking sheet.

4. Bake at 400° for 20 minutes or until puffy and golden brown. Remove from oven to a wire rack. Pierce 1 side of each cream puff with a knife to allow steam to escape. Cool completely on baking sheet (about 20 minutes).

5. Cut each cream puff in half horizontally. Scoop coffee ice cream onto bottom halves; top with remaining halves. Cover and freeze until ready to serve. Drizzle with hot fudge topping just before serving.

the scoop • • • • • • •

Use a 1-inch scoop coated with cooking spray to drop dough onto baking sheet. Store cooled, unfilled puffs in an airtight container up to 2 days.

These crunchy little meringue nests are great with many different combinations of ice cream, sorbet, and fruit, but they are divine with vanilla ice cream and lemony fresh raspberries.

MERINGUE NESTS WITH ICE CREAM AND RASPBERRIES

makes 6 servings   hands-on time 17 min.
total time 5 hours, 17 min.

Parchment paper
3   large egg whites
¼   tsp. cream of tartar
⅔   cup sugar
½   tsp. vanilla extract
2   cups fresh raspberries

1   Tbsp. sugar
1   Tbsp. fresh lemon juice
1½ cups vanilla ice cream
Garnishes: lemon zest and fresh
    mint sprigs

1. Preheat oven to 250°. Cover a large baking sheet with parchment paper. Draw 6 (4-inch) circles on parchment paper. Turn paper over.

2. Beat egg whites and cream of tartar at high speed with an electric mixer until foamy. Gradually add ⅔ cup sugar, 1 Tbsp. at a time, beating until stiff peaks form and sugar dissolves (about 2 to 4 minutes). Add vanilla extract; beat until blended.

3. Divide egg white mixture evenly among each of the 6 drawn circles, shaping meringues into nests with 1-inch sides using the back of a spoon.

4. Bake at 250° for 1 hour or until dry. Turn oven off; cool meringues in closed oven at least 4 hours.

5. Toss together raspberries, 1 Tbsp. sugar, and lemon juice in a small bowl. Let stand 1 hour. Carefully remove meringue nests from paper. Scoop ¼ cup ice cream into each meringue nest, and top evenly with raspberry mixture.

DIPPED ICE CREAM WHOOPIE PIES

makes 20 servings   hands-on time 23 min.
total time 2 hours, 48 min.

6 Tbsp. butter, softened
1 cup firmly packed light brown sugar
1 large egg
1¾ cups all-purpose flour
½ cup unsweetened cocoa
1½ tsp. baking powder
¼ tsp. table salt
¾ cup milk
Parchment paper
3 cups vanilla ice cream
12 oz. semisweet chocolate, chopped
Toppings: chocolate candy sprinkles, chopped pecans, sea salt, toffee bits, chopped almonds, flaked coconut

1. Preheat oven to 400°. Beat butter and brown sugar at medium speed with an electric mixer 3 minutes or until light and fluffy. Add egg, beating just until blended. Whisk together flour, cocoa, baking powder, and salt; add to butter mixture alternately with milk, beginning and ending with flour mixture. Beat at low speed just until blended after each addition, stopping to scrape bowl as needed.

2. Drop batter by tablespoonfuls 2 inches apart onto parchment paper-lined baking sheets. Bake at 400° for 8 minutes or until cookies spring back when lightly touched. Cool on pan 2 minutes; transfer to wire racks, and cool completely (about 15 minutes).

3. Spoon 2 Tbsp. ice cream onto flat side of half of cookies; top with remaining cookies. Place on a parchment paper-lined baking sheet. Freeze 1 hour.

4. Microwave chocolate in a small microwave-safe bowl at HIGH 1 to 2 minutes or until melted and smooth, stirring at 30-second intervals. Cool 5 minutes or until chocolate is barely warm to the touch. Dip frozen whoopie pies halfway into chocolate; immediately sprinkle with desired toppings. Return whoopie pies to baking sheet. Freeze 1 hour or until firm. Serve immediately, or wrap each whoopie pie individually with plastic wrap, and store in freezer up to 1 month.

These chocolate-cherry handfuls feature chocolate chunk-cherry ice cream sandwiched between brownie cookies packed with dried cherries. Say that three times fast!

CHOCOLATE-CHERRY ICE CREAM SANDWICHES

makes 15 servings   hands-on time 10 min.
total time 1 hour, 55 min.

2 Tbsp. vegetable oil	6 Tbsp. chopped dried cherries
1 large egg	Parchment paper
1 (18.75-oz.) package chocolate supreme brownie mix	5 cups cherry ice cream with chocolate chunks

1. Preheat oven to 325°. Whisk together oil, egg, and 2 Tbsp. water in medium bowl. Stir in brownie mix and cherries. Scoop batter into 30 (1-inch) balls using a small ice-cream or cookie scoop; place 2 inches apart on parchment paper-lined baking sheets.

2. Bake at 325° for 15 minutes or until set. Cool on pans 1 minute; transfer to wire racks, and cool completely (about 30 minutes).

3. Scoop ⅓ cup ice cream on flat side of each of 15 cookies; top each with another cookie, flat side down, pressing gently. Place ice-cream sandwiches on a parchment paper-lined baking sheet; freeze at least 1 hour or until firm. Serve immediately, or wrap each sandwich individually with plastic wrap, and store in freezer up to 1 month.

PEANUTTY ICE CREAM SANDWICHES

*makes 5 servings   hands-on time 15 min.
total time 1 hour, 45 min.*

½ cup chunky peanut butter
2 pints vanilla ice cream, softened

1 (8.75-oz.) package large chewy peanut butter cookies
1 cup coarsely chopped peanuts

1. Swirl peanut butter into softened ice cream. Freeze 30 minutes. Spread ice cream evenly on 1 side of 5 cookies; top with remaining cookies. Roll sides of sandwiches in coarsely chopped peanuts. Place in plastic or wax paper sandwich bags, and freeze at least 1 hour.

twist it up!

CHOCOLATE-MINT ICE CREAM SANDWICHES

Omit peanut butter and peanuts. Substitute 1 (8.5-oz) package large chewy chocolate cookies for chewy peanut butter cookies. Chop 15 mint-and-cream filled chocolate sandwich cookies; stir into softened ice cream, and proceed as directed.

With only five ingredients, you won't believe how decadent and satisfying these little treats can be. Take out of the freezer just before serving. They need to be super cold!

STRAWBERRY ICE CREAM SANDWICHES

makes 6 servings   hands-on time 10 min.
total time 2 hour, 10 min.

⅓ cup chopped fresh strawberries
2 Tbsp. strawberry preserves
12 devil's food cookie cakes

2 Tbsp. hot fudge topping
¾ cup strawberry ice cream

1. In small bowl, gently stir strawberries and preserves.

2. Place cookies, flat sides up, on work surface. Top each of 6 cookies with 1 tsp. fudge topping. Top each of remaining 6 cookies with 1 heaping tablespoon strawberry mixture and 2 Tbsp. ice cream. Place fudge-topped cookies, fudge side down, on ice cream; gently press together.

3. Place in plastic or wax paper sandwich bags. Freeze at least 2 hours or until firm.

the scoop • • • • • • •

If ice cream starts to melt while assembling these treats, keep sandwiches in freezer while working and remove only one at a time to fill.

LEMON BARS

makes 16 servings   hands-on time 24 min.
total time 7 hours, 24 min.

1   cup plus 1 Tbsp. sugar, divided
½   cup fresh lemon juice
6   large egg yolks
½   cup butter, cut into pieces
2   tsp. lemon zest
1   cup graham cracker crumbs
     (about 7 sheets)

3   Tbsp. butter, melted
⅛   tsp. table salt
4   cups lemon sorbet, softened
1   cup thawed whipped topping
16 small mint leaves (optional)

1. Whisk together 1 cup sugar, lemon juice, and egg yolks in a medium saucepan. Cook over low heat, whisking constantly, 8 to 10 minutes or until thickened. Remove from heat; add ½ cup butter and lemon zest, whisking until butter melts. Place heavy-duty plastic wrap directly on warm lemon curd (to prevent a film from forming); cool completely (about 1 hour).

2. Preheat oven to 350°. Line bottom and sides of an 8-inch square pan with aluminum foil, allowing 2 to 3 inches to extend over sides. Stir together graham cracker crumbs, remaining 1 Tbsp. sugar, 3 Tbsp. melted butter, and salt; press mixture in bottom of prepared pan. Bake at 350° for 10 to 12 minutes or until crust is lightly browned. Cool completely in pan on a wire rack (about 30 minutes).

3. Spread lemon sorbet evenly over prepared crust in pan. Spread lemon curd over sorbet. Place heavy-duty plastic wrap directly on surface of curd. Freeze 6 hours or until firm. Lift mixture from pan, using foil sides as handles. Cut into squares; top each serving with a dollop of whipped topping and, if desired, a mint leaf.

the scoop . . . .

If you are in a pinch for time, you can substitute 1⅓ cups bottled lemon curd for the homemade.

After cutting into bars, wrap any leftover treats individually in plastic wrap, and store in a zip-top plastic bag in the freezer. They'll be ready as a refresing treat on a warm day.

CHOCOLATE-DIPPED WAFFLE CONE BARS

makes 16 servings   hands-on time 17 min.
total time 7 hours, 12 min.

1	(7-oz.) package waffle cones, divided
¼	cup butter, melted
2	Tbsp. brown sugar
1	cup semisweet chocolate morsels
1	Tbsp. shortening
	Parchment paper
¾	cup toasted chopped pecans
5½	cups dulce de leche or caramel ice cream, softened

1. Preheat oven to 350°. Line bottom and sides of a 9-inch square pan with aluminum foil, allowing 2 to 3 inches to extend over sides. Break 8 waffle cones into pieces. Process waffle cone pieces, butter, and brown sugar in a food processor until finely crushed. Press crumb mixture into prepared pan.

2. Bake at 350° for 10 minutes. Cool completely in pan on a wire rack (about 30 minutes).

3. Break remaining 4 cones into 2-inch pieces. Microwave chocolate morsels and shortening in a small microwave-safe bowl at HIGH 1 to 1½ minutes or until melted, stirring at 30-second intervals. Dip waffle cone pieces entirely into melted chocolate; place on a parchment paper-lined baking sheet. Freeze 15 minutes.

4. Fold frozen waffle cone pieces and pecans into ice cream; spread evenly over crust.Cover and freeze 6 hours or until firm. Lift mixture from pan, using foil sides as handles. Cut into squares.

the scoop · · · · · · ·

To make these extra special, you can try this recipe using our home-made Dulce de Leche Ice Cream (page 197).

Perfect for kids, these treats can also be made with chocolate-flavored crisp rice cereal or rainbow-colored fruit-flavored crisp rice cereal and filled with their favorite ice cream.

CEREAL TREAT ICE CREAM SANDWICHES

makes 12 servings   hands-on time 13 min.
total time 4 hours, 33 min.

2 Tbsp. butter
4 cups miniature marshmallows, divided

3 cups crisp rice cereal
3 cups vanilla ice cream, softened

1. Line bottom and sides of 2 (8-inch) square pans with aluminum foil, allowing 2 to 3 inches to extend over sides; lightly grease foil.

2. Melt butter in a large saucepan over low heat. Add 3 cups marshmallows, stirring until melted. Remove from heat; stir in cereal. Quickly divide mixture evenly between prepared pans, pressing mixture in pans with wet hands. Cool completely in pans (about 20 minutes).

3. Lift cereal mixture from 1 pan, using foil sides as handles. Gently remove foil. Stir together remaining 1 cup marshmallows and ice cream; spread over cereal mixture in remaining pan. Place remaining cereal mixture over ice cream, pressing gently. Cover and freeze 4 hours or until firm.

4. Lift dessert from pan, using foil sides as handles. Cut into 12 ice-cream sandwiches. Serve immediately, or wrap each sandwich individually with plastic wrap, and store in freezer up to 1 month.

With so many yummy flavors of ice cream out there, it's fun to pick one with bits, pieces, and swirls to add to these sandwiches. Any caramel-swirled ice cream will work great with this recipe.

TOFFEE CRUNCH ICE CREAM SANDWICHES

makes 8 servings   hands-on time 15 min.   total time 1 hour, 30 min.

2 ⅔ cups English toffee and caramel swirl ice cream
16 pecan shortbread cookies

Parchment paper
3 (1.4-oz.) chocolate-covered toffee candy bars, finely chopped

1. Scoop ⅓ cup ice cream on flat side of each of 8 cookies; top each with another cookie, flat side down, pressing gently. Place ice-cream sandwiches on a parchment paper-lined baking sheet; freeze 15 minutes.

2. Place chopped candy bars in a shallow bowl. Roll sides of sandwiches in candy to coat ice cream; return sandwiches to baking sheet. Freeze at least 1 hour or until firm. Serve immediately, or wrap each sandwich individually with plastic wrap, and store in freezer up to 1 month.

note: We tested with Breyers Blasts! HEATH English Toffee Ice Cream.

MINI MOCHA ICE CREAM SCOOPS

makes 4 servings   hands-on time 20 min.   total time 1 hour

Parchment paper
½ cup chocolate-covered espresso beans
1¼ cups coffee or chocolate ice cream

1 (1-oz.) extra-dark chocolate square
4 sugar cones
2 Tbsp. shaved chocolate or chopped mixed nuts

1. Line a baking sheet with parchment paper, and place in freezer. Process espresso beans in a food processor 30 seconds or until finely chopped. Pour espresso crumbs into a shallow dish. Scoop ice cream into small balls using a 1¼-inch ice-cream or cookie scoop, and roll ice cream in espresso crumbs. Arrange on prepared baking sheet in freezer. Freeze 30 minutes to 24 hours.

2. Microwave chocolate square in a microwave-safe glass measuring cup at HIGH 1 minute or until melted, stirring at 30-second intervals. Dip top edges of 4 sugar cones into melted chocolate. Dip into shaved chocolate or chopped mixed nuts.

3. Serve ice-cream scoops in dipped sugar cones. Serve immediately, or wrap each cone individually with plastic wrap, and store in freezer up to 1 month.

twist it up!

MINI NUTTY ICE CREAM SCOOPS

Substitute ½ cup finely chopped mixed nuts for chocolate-covered espresso beans and low-fat vanilla bean ice cream for coffee ice cream. (Do not process nuts.)

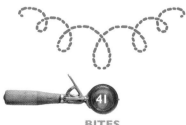

41

CARAMEL-ALMOND-VANILLA CONES

makes 6 servings   hands-on time 37 min.
total time 3 hours, 7 min.

3½ cups premium vanilla ice
     cream, divided
6   sugar cones
1   (11-oz.) package dry-roasted
     almonds, chopped (2¼ cups)

Parchment paper
2   (7.25-oz.) bottles caramel ice-
     cream shell topping

1. Let 1 cup plus 2 Tbsp. ice cream stand at room temperature 10 minutes to soften. (Keep remaining ice cream in freezer.) Spoon 3 Tbsp. softened ice cream into cavity of each cone, filling to top of cone; dip in chopped almonds. Place cones on a parchment paper-lined baking sheet, and freeze 30 minutes.

2. Scoop about ⅓ cup remaining ice cream on top of each cone. Return cones to baking sheet; freezet 1 hour.

3. Shake ice-cream shell topping; pour into a 2-cup glass measure. Working with 1 cone at a time (keep remaining cones in freezer), dip entire top of cone into shell topping, coating ice cream completely. Immediately dip into almonds. Return cone to baking sheet in freezer. Repeat procedure with remaining cones, shell topping, and almonds. Freeze at least 1 hour or until firm. Serve immediately, or wrap each cone individually with plastic wrap, and store in freezer up to 1 month.

OATMEAL-RUM-RAISIN ICE CREAM SANDWICHES

makes 5 servings   hands-on time 15 min.
total time 3 hours, 45 min.

¼   cup dark rum
½   cup golden raisins
2   pints vanilla ice cream, softened

1   (8.75-oz.) package large chewy
     oatmeal cookies

1. Pour rum over golden raisins; let stand 2 hours. Drain and discard rum. Stir rum-soaked raisins into softened ice cream. Freeze 30 minutes. Spread ice cream evenly on 1 side of 5 cookies; top with remaining cookies. Place in plastic or wax paper sandwich bags, and freeze at least 1 hour.

CHOCOLATE-HAZELNUT DIPPED CONES WITH SEA SALT

makes 6 servings   hands-on time 20 min.
total time 3 hours, 20 min.

6 large Styrofoam drinking cups
1 (4-oz.) bittersweet chocolate baking bar, chopped
1 Tbsp. hazelnut spread
2½ Tbsp. whipping cream
6 sugar cones

2 cups plus 6 Tbsp. chocolate ice cream
1 (7.25-oz.) bottle chocolate ice-cream shell topping
¼ cup toasted chopped hazelnuts
¼ tsp. sea salt

1. Cut bottoms out of Styrofoam drinking cups. Place cups upside down on a large baking sheet. Microwave chopped chocolate, hazelnut spread, and whipping cream in a small microwave-safe bowl at HIGH 1½ to 2 minutes or until melted and smooth, stirring at 30-second intervals. Spoon chocolate mixture evenly into cavities of cones. Place cones into holes in bottoms of cups so cones will stand upright.

2. Fill remainder of each cone cavity with about 1 Tbsp. ice cream. Scoop about ⅓ cup of ice cream on top of each cone; freeze 2 hours or until firm.

3. Shake shell topping, and drizzle over ice cream, covering as much as possible; immediately sprinkle with hazelnuts and sea salt. Freeze 1 hour before serving, or wrap each cone individually with plastic wrap, and store in freezer up to 1 month.

note: We tested with Nutella Hazelnut Spread.

ICE CREAM
SUNDAES

PILED HIGH, DRIZZLED, TOPPED,
AND SPRINKLED

CHERRY ICE CREAM CORDIALS

makes 4 servings   hands-on time 15 min.
total time 8 hours, 15 min.

½ cup maraschino cherries with stems

¼ cup Southern Comfort
Hot Fudge Ice Cream Topping, using bourbon (page 232)

2 cups cherry-vanilla ice cream
Garnishes: cherries with stems, sweetened whipped cream, chocolate sprinkles

1. Combine cherries and Southern Comfort; freeze in an airtight container 8 hours. Drain; pat cherries dry. Set aside 4 cherries for garnish. Discard stems from remaining cherries, and coarsely chop.

2. Layer Hot Fudge Ice Cream Topping, chopped cherries, and ice cream evenly in 4 small glasses.

Three mint ice creams and a rich hot fudge sauce combine to create a top-notch sundae. Garnish yours with your favorite toppings and make it a "just for you" treat.

TRIPLE MINT SUNDAES

makes 8 servings   hands-on time 10 min.   total time 20 min.

2 cups pink peppermint ice cream
2 cups mint-chocolate chip ice cream
2 cups spearmint ice cream

1 cup Hot Fudge Ice Cream Topping (page 232)
8 rolled wafer cookies
Garnish: fresh mint sprigs

1. Scoop ¼ cup each pink peppermint, mint-chocolate chip, and spearmint ice creams into julep cups or dessert glasses.

2. Drizzle each with 2 Tbsp. Hot Fudge Ice Cream Topping, and place a wafer cookie in each cup.

note: We tested with Pepperidge Farm Mint-Chocolate Pirouette Rolled Wafers.

the scoop • • • • • • •

Add a homemade touch by substituting Chocolate-Peppermint Ice Cream (page 196) for the store-bought pink peppermint ice cream.

Use vintage shot glasses for serving these mini indulgences. Get a head start by baking the candied pecans ahead, and then assemble the desserts in a snap.

CHOCOLATE-PRALINE SUNDAE SHOTS

makes 12 servings   hands-on time 11 min.   total time 23 min.

1 Tbsp. brown sugar	2½ cups butter pecan ice cream
1 tsp. butter, melted	½ cup hot fudge topping
12 pecan halves	

1. Preheat oven to 350°. Combine brown sugar and butter in a small bowl, stirring well. Add pecans; toss to coat. Spread pecans on an ungreased baking sheet. Bake at 350° for 12 minutes. Cool completely.

2. Using a 1 Tbsp. cookie scoop, place 2 ice-cream scoops into each of 12 chilled tiny dessert or shot glasses. Top each dessert with 2 tsp. room-temperature hot fudge topping and either a praline pecan half or chopped praline pecans. Serve immediately.

COOKIE BOX SUNDAES

makes 4 servings   hands-on time 15 min.
total time 2 hours, 25 min.

2   cups coffee ice cream
16   square butter cookies

½   cup Espresso-Hot Fudge Sauce
Garnish: fresh strawberries

1. Place 4 (¼-cup) scoops of ice cream onto a cold jelly-roll pan; freeze 2 hours. Press 4 butter cookies onto sides of each scoop, forming a box. Top each with 1 (¼-cup) scoop of ice cream. Freeze up to 2 hours. Serve with Espresso-Hot Fudge Sauce.

note: We tested with Pepperidge Farm Chessmen Cookies.

ESPRESSO-HOT FUDGE SAUCE

Melt 1 (8-oz.) package unsweetened chocolate baking squares and ½ cup butter in a large, heavy saucepan over low heat, stirring constantly. Add 2 cups sugar and 2 Tbsp. instant espresso, and cook, stirring constantly, 30 seconds or until blended. Add 1 cup milk, and cook, stirring constantly, 3 minutes or until thoroughly heated and sugar is dissolved. (Do not boil.) Remove from heat. Stir in 1 tsp. vanilla extract and ⅛ tsp. table salt. Use immediately, or cover and chill sauce up to 2 weeks. Makes 3¼ cups.

CHOCOLATE-ALMOND BISCOTTI SUNDAE

makes 4 servings   hands-on time 17 min.   total time 17 min.

- ¾ **cup whipping cream**
- 2 **Tbsp. amaretto liqueur or almond liqueur**
- 1 **Tbsp. powdered sugar**
- 3 **cups chocolate ice cream with roasted almonds**
- 12 **dark chocolate-dipped almond biscotti bites, cut in half**
- ⅔ **cup Hot Fudge Ice Cream Topping (page 232)**
- ⅓ **cup chocolate-covered almonds, chopped**

1. Beat whipping cream, amaretto, and powdered sugar in a medium bowl at medium speed with an electric mixer until stiff peaks form. Cover and chill until ready to serve.

2. Scoop ¾ cup ice cream into each of 4 bowls. Place 6 biscotti halves in each bowl; drizzle with Hot Fudge Ice Cream Topping. Top each serving with whipped cream, and sprinkle with almonds.

note: We tested with Nonni's Almond Dark chocolate biscotti bites.

the scoop

If you can't find biscotti bites, cut larger biscotti into 1-inch pieces. Also, substitute store-bought hot fudge topping for an even faster sundae.

RED VELVET-BERRY COBBLER SUNDAE

makes 6 to 8 servings   hands-on time 20 min.
total time 1 hour, 15 min.

1 Tbsp. cornstarch	1 tsp. vanilla extract
1¼ cups sugar, divided	1¼ cups all-purpose flour
8 cups assorted fresh berries, divided (We used 3 cups each raspberries and blueberries, and 2 cups blackberries.)	1½ Tbsp. unsweetened cocoa
	¼ tsp. table salt
	½ cup buttermilk
	1½ tsp. white vinegar
½ cup butter, softened	½ tsp. baking soda
2 large eggs	Cream Cheese Ice Cream (page 186)
2 Tbsp. red liquid food coloring	Garnish: fresh mint sprigs

1. Preheat oven to 350°. Stir together cornstarch and ½ cup sugar. Toss 6 cups berries with cornstarch mixture, and spoon into a lightly greased 11- x 7-inch baking dish.

2. Beat butter at medium speed with an electric mixer until fluffy; gradually add remaining ¾ cup sugar, beating well. Add eggs, 1 at a time, beating just until blended after each addition. Stir in red food coloring and vanilla until blended.

3. Combine flour, cocoa, and salt. Stir together buttermilk, vinegar, and baking soda in a 2-cup liquid measuring cup. (Mixture will bubble.) Add flour mixture to butter mixture alternately with buttermilk mixture, beginning and ending with flour mixture. Beat at low speed until blended after each addition. Spoon batter over berry mixture.

4. Bake at 350° for 45 to 50 minutes or until a wooden pick inserted in center of cake topping comes out clean. Cool on a wire rack 10 minutes.

5. Top scoops of cobbler with ice cream and remaining 2 cups fresh berries.

STRAWBERRY MANGO-MINT SUNDAES

makes 4 servings   hands-on time 15 min.   total time 15 min.

2	cups chopped peeled mango	2	cups sliced fresh strawberries
2	Tbsp. agave nectar or honey	1⅓	cups vanilla ice cream
2	Tbsp. chopped fresh mint leaves	8	tsp. chopped toasted pistachios

1. In food processor, place 1 cup mango and agave nectar. Cover; process until smooth. Stir in mint.

2. In medium bowl, gently toss together remaining 1 cup mango, strawberries, and mango-mint sauce.

3. Spoon 1 cup strawberry mixture into each of 4 dessert dishes; top each with ⅓ cup ice cream and 2 tsp. pistachios.

CREAM CHEESE BROWNIE SUNDAES

makes 12 servings   hands-on time 15 min.   total time 50 min.

1 (18.25-oz.) box chocolate cake mix
3 large eggs
½ cup butter, melted
1 (8-oz.) package cream cheese, softened

1 (16-oz.) box powdered sugar
⅓ cup unsweetened cocoa
4 cups mint-chocolate chip ice cream
1½ cups hot fudge topping

1. Preheat oven to 350°. Beat cake mix, 1 egg, and butter at medium speed with an electric mixer until combined. Press mixture into bottom of a lightly greased 13- x 9-inch baking dish.

2. Beat cream cheese and sugar at medium speed with an electric mixer until smooth. Add remaining 2 eggs, 1 at a time, beating well after each addition. Gradually add cocoa, beating until blended. Pour mixture evenly over chocolate layer.

3. Bake at 350° for 35 to 40 minutes or until a wooden pick inserted in center comes out clean. Cool completely. Cut into squares.

4. Place brownies in serving bowls, top each with ⅓ cup ice cream and 2 Tbsp. fudge topping.

the scoop · · · · · · ·

Instead of mint-chocolate chip ice cream, try serving these sundaes with Cream Cheese Ice Cream (page 186).

MINT-HOT FUDGE BROWNIE SUNDAES

MINT-CHOCOLATE SAUCE

1. Microwave 1 (12-oz.) can evaporated milk in a microwave-safe bowl at HIGH 2 minutes or until hot. Stir in 8 oz. crushed hard peppermint candies (about 45 candies), stirring constantly until candies dissolve.

2. Melt 4 (1-oz.) squares unsweetened chocolate and ½ cup butter in a large heavy saucepan over low heat, stirring constantly. Gradually stir in evaporated milk mixture. Gradually whisk in ½ cup sugar.

3. Cook, whisking constantly, over low heat 3 minutes or until smooth. Remove from heat, and whisk in ⅛ tsp. table salt. Makes 3½ cups.

makes 8 servings   hands-on time 10 min.
total time 20 min.

8	(3-inch-square) prepared brownies	2	cups Mint-Chocolate Sauce
4	cups vanilla ice cream		Garnish: crushed hard peppermint candies

1. Place 1 brownie in each of 8 sundae dishes; top each with 2 scoops vanilla ice cream and ¼ cup Mint-Chocolate Sauce.

the scoop

To crush the peppermint candies, unwrap them, place in a large zip-top plastic bag, and seal. Bash the candies with a rolling pin until coarsely chopped.

PEANUT BRITTLE-BUTTERSCOTCH SUNDAES

makes 4 servings   hands-on time 17 min.   total time 32 min.

Parchment paper
Vegetable cooking spray
1   cup sugar
1   cup light corn syrup
2   Tbsp. butter
½   tsp. baking soda
1½ cups dry-roasted peanuts

½   tsp. coarse sea salt
4   cups vanilla bean ice cream
1   (12.25-oz.) jar butterscotch
    topping
¾   cup whipping cream, whipped

1. Line a baking sheet with parchment paper, and heavily coat paper with vegetable cooking spray.

2. Combine sugar, corn syrup, and ½ cup water in a medium-size heavy saucepan; cook over medium heat, whisking often, 8 to 10 minutes or until sugar caramelizes. Remove from heat; add butter, stirring until butter melts. Stir in baking soda until blended. Quickly stir in peanuts (mixture will foam up). Immediately pour mixture onto prepared baking sheet, spreading to ¼-inch thickness; sprinkle with salt. Cool 15 minutes or until firm. Break into pieces.

3. Scoop 1 cup ice cream into each of 4 sundae glasses; drizzle each sundae with ¼ cup butterscotch topping, and sprinkle each with ⅓ cup peanut brittle. Top evenly with whipped cream; drizzle evenly with remaining butterscotch topping. Sprinkle with additional peanut brittle, if desired.

the scoop • • • • • • •

Try this sundae with **Salted Bourbon-Spiked Toffee Sauce (page 230)** instead of using store-bought topping.

BANANA-BERRY SPLIT

makes 2 to 4 servings   hands-on time 5 min.   total time 15 min.

2	medium-size ripe bananas, sliced in half lengthwise	½	pt. fresh blackberries
6	scoops strawberry ice cream	½	pt. fresh raspberries
½	cup Hot Fudge Ice Cream Topping (page 232)	½	pt. fresh blueberries
		½	cup chopped salted peanuts
			Garnish: fresh mint sprigs

1. Place two banana halves in a serving dish; add 3 scoops strawberry ice cream between banana halves. Top with half each of Hot Fudge Ice Cream Topping, blackberries, raspberries, blueberries, and peanuts. Repeat procedure with remaining ingredients.

the scoop . . . .

If you make the Hot Fudge Ice Cream Topping (page 232) in advance and refrigerate it, simply reheat the amount needed in the microwave.

Give these sundaes a campfire flavor by topping with marshmallow crème and then toasting with a small kitchen torch. Top with with chocolate morsels and graham cracker sticks.

S'MORES SUNDAES

makes 4 servings   hands-on time 10 min.   total time 1 hour, 10 min.

2   cups chocolate chunk ice cream, slightly softened
20 graham cracker sticks, crushed
¼   cup marshmallow crème

4   tsp. semisweet chocolate mini-morsels
8   whole graham cracker sticks

1. Stir together softened ice cream and crushed graham crackers in a small bowl. Freeze 1 hour or until firm.

2. Spoon ice cream mixture into 4 bowls; top evenly with marshmallow crème and chocolate morsels. Serve each with 2 graham cracker sticks.

note: We tested with Honey Maid Grahams Honey Sticks.

This ruby-colored adult sundae is fancy enough for dinner parties with the addition of chocolate and black raspberry liqueurs and a touch of brandy.

CHERRIES JUBILEE

makes 6 servings   hands-on time 10 min.   total time 15 min.

1   (15-oz.) can pitted Bing cherries in syrup
1   (14.5-oz.) can pitted tart cherries in water
2   Tbsp. cornstarch
¼   cup sugar
½   tsp. ground allspice

¼   cup black raspberry liqueur
¼   cup brandy
6   Tbsp. chocolate liqueur
1   qt. vanilla ice cream
12 chocolate fudge cream-filled rolled wafers

1. Combine cherries in a heavy non-aluminum 3-qt. saucepan; reserve 6 Tbsp. syrup. Stir together cornstarch and reserved syrup.

2. Stir together sugar and allspice; add to cherries, and bring to a boil over medium heat. Reduce heat to low; add cornstarch mixture, and cook, stirring constantly, 2 to 3 minutes or until mixture is thickened and slightly clear. Remove from heat. Stir in raspberry liqueur and brandy; return to heat, and cook over medium heat, stirring constantly, 1 minute.

3. Place 1 Tbsp. chocolate liqueur in each of 6 (6-oz.) serving dishes, and top with 1 scoop ice cream. Pour cherry mixture evenly over ice cream in each dish, and serve with 2 chocolate wafers.

note: We tested with Chambord Black Raspberry Liqueur, Godiva Original Chocolate Liqueur, and Pepperidge Farm Chocolate Fudge Crème-Filled Pirouette Rolled Wafers.

This multi-layered sundae is like having breakfast for dessert. Waffles, pecans, and ice cream are drizzled with a bourbon-toffee sauce and sprinkled with bacon pieces!

BOURBON-PECAN WAFFLE SUNDAES

makes 4 servings hands-on time 15 min. total time 23 min.

4   frozen Belgian waffles
2   cups pecan pralines 'n' cream
     ice cream
¾   cup Salted Bourbon-Spiked
     Toffee Sauce (page 230)

Refrigerated instant whipped cream
¼   cup chopped toasted pecans
4   cooked and crumbled bacon
     slices

1. Preheat oven to 425°.

2. Arrange waffles on a wire rack in a jelly-roll pan. Bake at 425° for 8 minutes or until toasted. Remove waffles from oven; cool 5 minutes.

3. Place waffles on each of 4 plates; top each waffle with a scoop of ice cream. Drizzle sundaes evenly with Salted Bourbon-Spiked Toffee Sauce; top evenly with whipped cream, pecans, and bacon.

note: We tested with Van's Belgian Waffles and Blue Bell Pecan Pralines 'n' Cream Ice Cream.

Store-bought cookie dough gets baked in individual dishes to make for the most indulgent ice-cream bowl imaginable! Top them off with peanuts, whipped cream, and hot fudge.

WARM PEANUT BUTTER COOKIE SUNDAES

makes 6 servings   hands-on time 10 min.   total time 40 min.

6   packaged ready-to-bake peanut butter cookie dough rounds with mini peanut butter cups

2   cups vanilla ice cream
Toppings: hot fudge sauce, whipped cream, chopped peanuts

1. Preheat oven to 350°.

2. Place each cookie dough round into a lightly greased 8-oz. ramekin or individual soufflé dish. Bake at 350° for 25 to 30 minutes or until cookies are lightly browned. Cool 5 minutes.

3. Scoop vanilla ice cream evenly into each ramekin, and top sundaes with desired toppings. Serve immediately.

note: We tested with half of an 18-oz. package of Pillsbury Ready Bake Peanut Butter Cup Cookies.

the scoop . . . .

We liked the cookie cups soft, but for a crispier cookie, increase the bake time.

This fancy restaurant-worthy dessert dresses up vanilla ice cream with warm, rum-soaked caramelized bananas. Eat fast—it melts quickly!

BANANAS FOSTER

makes 6 to 8 servings   hands-on time 10 min.   total time 10 min.

4	medium-size ripe bananas	¼	cup banana liqueur
½	cup butter	½	cup rum
1	cup firmly packed brown sugar	6	cups vanilla ice cream

1. Cut bananas in half crosswise; cut each half in half lengthwise. Melt butter in a large skillet over medium-high heat; add brown sugar, and cook, stirring constantly, 2 minutes.

2. Add bananas to skillet, and remove from heat. Stir in liqueur and rum, and carefully ignite fumes just above mixture with a long match or long multipurpose lighter. Let flames die down.

3. Return skillet to heat, and cook 3 to 4 minutes or until bananas are soft and curl slightly. Remove from heat. Serve banana mixture immediately over scoops of vanilla ice cream.

the scoop . . . .

Pre-scoop the ice cream into a large bowl, and store it in the freezer to make serving fast and easy.

Coffee ice cream is nestled in a homemade chocolate meringue bowl, topped with cookie crumbs and toasted pecans, and drizzled with chocolate syrup to make the ultimate dessert experience.

MUD PIE MERINGUE SUNDAES

makes 6 servings   hands-on time 20 min.
total time 13 hours, 50 min.

Parchment paper
3   large egg whites (at room temperature)
½   tsp. vanilla extract
⅛   tsp. cream of tartar
½   cup sugar

2   Tbsp. sifted unsweetened cocoa
2   cups coffee ice cream
4   cream-filled chocolate sandwich cookies, crushed
2   Tbsp. chopped toasted pecans
3   Tbsp. chocolate sundae syrup

1. Preheat oven to 225°. Cover a large baking sheet with parchment paper. Draw 6 (3-inch) circles on paper. Turn paper over; secure with masking tape.

2. Place egg whites, vanilla, and cream of tartar in a large bowl; beat at high speed with an electric mixer until foamy. Gradually add sugar, 1 Tbsp. at a time, beating mixture until stiff peaks form. Gently fold in cocoa.

3. Divide egg white mixture evenly among the 6 drawn circles. Shape meringues into nests with 1-inch sides using the back of a spoon.

4. Bake at 225° for 1½ hours or until dry. Turn oven off, and cool meringues in closed oven at least 12 hours. Remove from oven; carefully remove meringues from paper.

5. Place meringues on individual dessert plates. Top each with ⅓ cup ice cream. Sprinkle each evenly with 1½ Tbsp. cookie crumbs and 1 tsp. pecans; drizzle each with 1½ tsp. chocolate syrup. Serve immediately.

DESSERT TACOS

makes 4 servings   hands-on time 10 min.   total time 20 min.

1	Tbsp. sugar	2	kiwifruit, peeled and sliced
¼	tsp. ground cinnamon	1	pt. strawberries, sliced
4	(8-inch) flour tortillas	¼	cup toasted coconut flakes
1	Tbsp. butter, melted		
2	cups chocolate ice cream		

1. Preheat oven to 350°. Combine sugar and cinnamon. Brush tortillas with melted butter; sprinkle evenly with sugar mixture.

2. Shape 4 sheets of aluminum foil into 4-inch balls on a baking sheet. Place tortillas, butter side down, over foil balls; press to resemble taco shells.

3. Bake at 350° for 10 minutes or until crisp. Cool completely on foil on baking sheet. Remove tortillas, and fill evenly with chocolate ice cream, kiwifruit, strawberries, and coconut.

When you can't decide between pumpkin pie and pecan pie and you love ice cream, this is your fantasy dessert! It literally uses a whole pumpkin pie!

PUMPKIN PIE ICE CREAM FANTASY

makes 12 servings   hands-on time 10 min.   total time 20 min.

1 baked pumpkin pie	1½ cups caramel topping
½ gal. premium vanilla ice cream	1½ cups toasted pecan halves

1. Place pie in freezer for 1 hour; remove pie from freezer, and chop ¾ of pie into 1-inch chunks. Allow ice cream to stand about 8 to 10 minutes to slightly soften. Scoop ice cream into a large bowl. Gently fold in pumpkin pie chunks until blended.

2. To serve, scoop each serving of ice cream into dessert bowls. Drizzle each with 2 Tbsp. caramel topping, and top with 2 Tbsp. pecans.

note: We tested with a Mrs. Smith's Frozen Pumpkin Pie (baked according to package directions), Blue Bell Premium Vanilla Ice Cream, and Smucker's Caramel Topping.

the scoop

You can use any type of pumpkin pie for this recipe—a deli-baked pie or, better yet, a home-made pie. In fact, a pecan pie would be a delicious choice. Just omit the toasted pecan halves.

76

SCOOPED

THE COOLEST TARTS AND THE PRETTIEST PIES

PISTACHIO-CHERRY TART

makes 8 servings   hands-on time 12 min.   total time 5 hours, 4 min.

30 chocolate wafers, finely crushed (about 1½ cups)
¼ cup sugar
¼ cup butter, melted
¼ tsp. table salt

6 oz. bittersweet chocolate, chopped
1 (12-oz.) package frozen dark, sweet pitted cherries (2 cups), thawed and drained
1 pt. pistachio ice cream, softened

1. Preheat oven to 350°. Stir together first 4 ingredients in a medium bowl; press mixture onto bottom and up sides of a 9-inch tart pan with removable bottom.

2. Bake at 350° for 10 to 12 minutes. Cool completely on a wire rack (about 30 minutes).

3. Microwave chocolate in a small microwave-safe bowl at HIGH 1 to 1½ minutes or until melted and smooth, stirring at 30-second intervals. Spoon ⅓ cup melted chocolate into bottom of cooled crust, spreading evenly. Freeze 10 minutes or until set.

4. Coarsely chop cherries, and fold into pistachio ice cream. Spoon mixture into crust, spreading evenly. Drizzle with remaining melted chocolate. Cover and freeze 4 hours until firm.

CARAMEL-APPLE ICE CREAM TARTS

makes 8 servings   hands-on time 30 min.
total time 6 hours, 5 min.

CARAMELIZED APPLE CHIPS

1. Preheat oven to 350°. Place a lightly greased wire rack in an aluminum foil-lined 15- x 10-inch jelly-roll pan. Cut 1 small apple into ⅙-inch-thick slices, cutting through stem and bottom end using a mandoline.

2. Bring 1 cup sugar and 1 cup water to a boil in a 3-qt. sauce-pan over medium-high heat, stirring constantly. Add apple slices, and cook, stirring often, 10 to 12 minutes or until apples are slightly translucent. Quickly remove apples from syrup; transfer to wire rack in pan.

3. Bake at 350° for 10 to 15 minutes or until golden; remove from oven, and transfer apples to lightly greased wax paper, using tongs. Cool completely. Makes about 2 dozen.

1⅔ cups all-purpose flour
¾ cup butter, cubed
⅔ cup powdered sugar
⅓ cup cornstarch
2 Tbsp. butter
2 cups peeled and diced Gala apples
⅓ cup firmly packed light brown sugar
2 Tbsp. bourbon
2 pt. vanilla ice cream
1 recipe Caramel Sauce (page 229)
½ cup lightly salted roasted pecans
Garnish: Caramelized Apple Chips

1. Preheat oven to 350°. Pulse first 4 ingredients in a food processor 10 to 12 times or until mixture resembles coarse meal. Firmly press on bottom and up sides of 8 (3¾-inch) round tart pans with removable bottoms (about 7 Tbsp. per pan). Place tart pans on a baking sheet. Bake 25 to 30 minutes or until lightly browned. Cool completely on baking sheet on a wire rack (about 30 minutes).

2. Melt 2 Tbsp. butter in a large skillet over medium-high heat; add apples and brown sugar. Cook, stirring constantly, 8 to 10 minutes or until tender and caramelized. Remove from heat, and stir in bourbon. Cool completely (about 30 minutes).

3. Let ice cream stand at room temperature 10 minutes or until softened; place ice cream in a large bowl, and stir in apple mixture. Cover and freeze 4 hours or until firm. Serve in tart shells with Caramel Sauce and pecans.

LEMON MERINGUE ICE CREAM PIE

makes 8 servings   hands-on time 15 min.
total time 9 hours, 55 min.

2   pt. vanilla ice cream
1   (9-inch deep-dish) Vanilla
    Wafer Crust (page 245)
1½ cups store-bought lemon
    curd

16 vanilla wafers
    Meringue Topping

1. Let ice cream stand at room temperature 5 minutes or just until soft enough to spread. Spoon 1 pt. ice cream into Vanilla Wafer Crust. Top with ¾ cup lemon curd; repeat with remaining ice cream and lemon curd. Gently swirl ice cream and curd with a knife or small spatula. Insert vanilla wafers around edge of pie. Cover and freeze 8 hours.

2. Spread Meringue Topping over pie. If desired, brown meringue using a kitchen torch, holding torch 1 to 2 inches from pie and moving torch back and forth. (If you do not have a torch, preheat broiler with oven rack 8 inches from heat; broil 30 to 45 seconds or until golden.) Serve immediately, or cover loosely with plastic wrap, and freeze 4 hours or up to 1 week.

MERINGUE TOPPING

1. Pour water to depth of 1½ inches into a 3½-qt. saucepan; bring to a boil over medium-high heat. Reduce heat to medium, and let simmer.

2. Meanwhile, combine 2 egg whites, 1¼ cups sugar, 1 Tbsp. light corn syrup, 1 tsp. vanilla extract, and ¼ cup water in a 2½-qt. glass bowl; beat mixture at high speed with an electric mixer until blended.

3. Place bowl over simmering water, and beat at high speed 5 to 7 minutes or until soft peaks form; remove from heat. Beat to spreading consistency (about 2 to 3 minutes). Use immediately. Makes about 4 cups.

85

PIES

You'll go bananas over this delicious pie featuring a vanilla wafer crust, fresh bananas, and caramel topping layered with ice cream and finished with fluffy rum-spiked whipped cream.

BANANAS FOSTER PIE

makes 8 to 10 servings   hands-on time 16 min.
total time 6 hours, 58 min.

¾	cup caramel topping, divided	4	cups vanilla ice cream, softened
1	(9-inch deep-dish) Vanilla Wafer Crust (page 245)	2	cups whipping cream
		6	Tbsp. powdered sugar
3	medium-size ripe bananas, sliced	2	Tbsp. dark rum

1. Spread ¼ cup caramel topping over bottom of Vanilla Wafer Crust. Arrange 1½ sliced bananas over caramel. Spread 2 cups ice cream over bananas. Repeat layers, working quickly. Cover and freeze 6 hours or until firm.

2. Beat whipping cream at high speed with an electric mixer until foamy; gradually add powdered sugar, beating until soft peaks form. Add dark rum; beat just until blended. Spread whipped cream over pie; drizzle with remaining ¼ cup caramel topping. Serve immediately.

the scoop • • • • • • •

If desired, replace the store-bought vanilla ice cream with store-bought caramel ice cream or with Bananas Foster Ice Cream (page 191).

The striking look of this cookie pie is sure to wow your family and friends. The hidden chocolate layer is a surprise treat in every delicious bite.

BLACK & WHITE ICE CREAM COOKIE PIE

makes 8 servings   hands-on time 13 min.
total time 7 hours, 3 min.

⅓ cup semisweet chocolate morsels
⅓ cup sweetened condensed milk
1½ tsp. unsweetened cocoa
2 Tbsp. butter
½ tsp. vanilla extract
1 (9-inch) Chocolate-Cream Cookie Crust (page 244)
4 cups cookies-and-cream ice cream, softened

14 cream-filled vanilla sandwich cookies, divided
14 cream-filled chocolate sandwich cookies, divided
1 (8-oz.) container frozen whipped topping, thawed

1. Stir together chocolate morsels, sweetened condensed milk, cocoa, and 2 Tbsp. butter in a medium saucepan over medium heat until chocolate is melted and mixture is smooth. Remove from heat; stir in vanilla. Cool 30 minutes or to room temperature.

2. Spread chocolate sauce over Chocolate-Cream Cookie Crust; freeze 10 minutes. Spread ice cream over chocolate sauce; arrange 8 vanilla sandwich cookies and 8 chocolate sandwich cookies around outside edge of pie, alternating chocolate and vanilla cookies and gently pressing cookies into ice cream. Spread whipped topping over pie; place pie in freezer.

3. Place remaining 6 vanilla sandwich cookies in a zip-top plastic freezer bag; crush cookies using a meat mallet or rolling pin. Sprinkle crushed cookies on half of pie, and return to freezer. Repeat procedure with remaining 6 chocolate sandwich cookies; sprinkle chocolate crumbs on other half of pie. Freeze 6 hours or until firm. Let stand 10 minutes before slicing.

Good local honey and peak-of-the-season peaches are key players in the flavor of this summertime pie. A touch of lemon juice brings out the fresh peach flavor.

PEACH-HONEY ICEBOX PIE

*makes 8 servings   hands-on time 17 min.
total time 9 hours, 47 min.*

¼   cup butter
2½   cups chopped fresh or frozen peaches, thawed
¼   cup plus 3 Tbsp. good-quality local honey, divided
1   Tbsp. fresh lemon juice
2   cups vanilla ice cream, softened
1   (9-inch) ready-made graham cracker piecrust
1   cup whipping cream
Garnish: fresh mint sprigs, chopped fresh peaches

1. Melt butter in a large skillet over medium heat. Add peaches and ¼ cup honey; cook, stirring often, 6 minutes or until peaches have softened and liquid has thickened to a syrup that coats peaches. Spoon peach mixture into a medium bowl; place over a bowl of ice, and stir occasionally until cool (about 1 hour). Stir in lemon juice.

2. Add vanilla ice cream to peach mixture; stir well. Spoon ice-cream mixture into crust, spreading evenly. Cover and freeze 6 hours or until firm.

3. Let pie stand at room temperature 15 minutes before serving. Meanwhile, beat whipping cream at high speed with an electric mixer until stiff peaks form. Spoon whipped cream over pie, and drizzle with remaining 3 Tbsp. honey.

the scoop • • • • • • •

Make a Graham Cracker Crust (page 246) from scratch instead of using the store-bought variety, if you have a little extra time.

KEY LIME ICE CREAM PIE

makes 8 servings hands-on time 20 min. total time 1 hour, 10 min.

1 (10-oz.) jar lemon curd
1 (9-inch) Buttery Cookie Crust (page 246)
1 recipe Avocado-Key Lime Pie Ice Cream (page 201)

2 cups whipping cream
¼ cup powdered sugar
⅛ tsp. coconut extract
Garnishes: macadamia nuts, toasted coconut curls, Key lime zest

1. Spread half of lemon curd on bottom of Buttery Cookie Crust, and freeze 10 minutes. Spread half of Avocado-Key Lime Pie Ice Cream over lemon curd; freeze 15 minutes. Repeat layers with remaining lemon curd and remaining ice cream, freezing as directed above after each layer.

2. Beat whipping cream, powdered sugar, and coconut extract at medium speed with an electric mixer until soft peaks form; spread over top of pie.

Fresh mint and strawberries are a classic summertime combination. Whirred up with frozen yogurt and served in a chocolatey crust you can't go wrong!

CREAMY STRAWBERRY-MINT PIE

makes 10 servings   hands-on time 30 min.   total time 4 hours, 45 min.

1   qt. strawberry frozen yogurt
1   (16-oz.) package fresh strawberries, hulled
2   Tbsp. powdered sugar
2   Tbsp. chopped fresh mint

1   (9-inch) Chocolate-Cream Cookie Crust (page 244), baked in a spring-form pan
Garnishes: fresh strawberries slices, fresh mint, Fresh Strawberry Syrup (page 226)

1. Let frozen yogurt stand at room temperature 20 minutes or until slightly softened. Process strawberries, powdered sugar, and mint in food processor until strawberries are pureed, stopping to scrape down sides as needed.

2. Place frozen yogurt in a large bowl; cut into large (3-inch) pieces. Fold strawberry mixture into yogurt until smooth. Spoon mixture into Chocolate-Cream Cookie Crust. Freeze 3 hours or until firm. Let stand at room temperature 15 minutes before serving.

BLUEBERRY CHEESECAKE ICE CREAM PIE

makes 8 to 10 servings   hands-on time 30 min.
total time 2 hours

½   cup blueberry preserves
1   (9-inch) Shortbread Cookie
    Crust
1   recipe Blueberry Cheese-
    cake Ice Cream (page 199)

Toppings: sweetened whipped
    cream, fresh blueberries and
    blackberries, lemon zest twists,
    fresh mint sprigs

1. Spread ¼ cup blueberry preserves on bottom of crust, and freeze 10 minutes. Spread half of ice cream over preserves, and freeze 15 minutes. Repeat layers once with remaining ¼ cup preserves and remaining ice cream, freezing as directed above after each layer.

2. Top with desired toppings.

SHORTBREAD COOKIE CRUST

Process 1 (10-oz.) package shortbread cookies in a food processor until finely ground. Stir together shortbread crumbs and ¼ cup melted butter. Press mixture on bottom and up sides of a lightly greased 9-inch pie plate. Freeze 30 minutes or until set. Makes 1 (9-inch) crust.

note: We tested with Smucker's Blueberry Preserves and Nabisco Lorna Doone Shortbread Cookies.

We turned everyone's favorite ice-cream truck treat into an outrageous frozen pie, complete with waffle cones on top, caramel and vanilla gelato, and a homemade caramel topping.

CARAMEL CONE ICE CREAM PIE

makes 10 to 12 servings   hands-on time 30 min.
total time 11 hours, 10 min.

⅔ cup jarred dark chocolate topping, divided

1 cup jarred butterscotch-caramel topping, divided

1 (9-inch) No-Bake Chocolate Wafer Crust (page 245)

6 waffle cones, divided

1 pt. vanilla bean gelato, softened

1 pt. sea salt-caramel gelato, softened

1 cup heavy cream

2 Tbsp. light brown sugar

1 tsp. vanilla extract

Garnish: shaved chocolate

1. Drizzle ⅓ cup chocolate topping and ⅓ cup butterscotch-caramel topping onto bottom of No-Bake Chocolate Wafer Crust. Crush 2 waffle cones, and sprinkle over toppings, pressing lightly to adhere. Freeze 30 minutes.

2. Spread vanilla gelato over crushed cones; drizzle with ⅓ cup butterscotch-caramel topping and remaining chocolate topping. Crush 2 waffle cones, and sprinkle over toppings; freeze 30 minutes. Spread caramel gelato over crushed cones. Cover and freeze 8 hours.

3. Beat cream, brown sugar, and vanilla extract at medium speed with an electric mixer until soft peaks form. Dollop whipped cream over pie; break remaining 2 waffle cones into large pieces, and arrange on top of pie. Cover and freeze 1 hour or until whipped cream is firm. Drizzle with remaining ⅓ cup butterscotch-caramel topping, and let stand 10 to 15 minutes before serving.

note: We tested with Smucker's Special Recipe Toppings.

We've taken the soda-shop classic and turned it into an eye-popping fun pie—with a cherry on top! A handful of rainbow sprinkles and fresh whipped cream makes this a crowd favorite.

ICE CREAM SUNDAE PIE

makes 6 to 8 servings hands-on time 10 min.
total time 6 hours, 40 min.

¾ cup chocolate-hazelnut spread, divided

1 (6-oz.) ready-made chocolate crumb piecrust

2 small ripe bananas, sliced

1 pt. chocolate ice cream, softened

2 pt. vanilla ice cream, softened

1½ cups whipping cream

2 Tbsp. sugar

¼ cup multi-colored sprinkles

¼ cup maraschino cherries with stems

1. Dollop ½ cup chocolate-hazelnut spread over bottom of crust; gently spread to cover bottom of crust. Arrange bananas over chocolate-hazelnut spread. Spoon chocolate ice cream over bananas, spreading evenly. Scoop vanilla ice cream onto pie, leaving scoop shapes intact. Cover and freeze 6 hours or until firm.

2. Let pie stand at room temperature 10 minutes before serving. Meanwhile, beat whipping cream and sugar at high speed with an electric mixer until stiff peaks form; dollop or pipe over pie.

3. Spoon remaining ¼ cup chocolate-hazelnut spread into a small zip-top plastic bag (do not seal). Snip 1 corner of bag to make a small hole; drizzle chocolate-hazelnut spread over pie. Sprinkle with sprinkles and cherries.

note: We tested with Keebler Chocolate Ready Crust.

the scoop . . . .

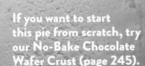

If you want to start this pie from scratch, try our No-Bake Chocolate Wafer Crust (page 245).

The salty pretzel crust mimics the salted rim on a margarita glass. With a touch of tequila and orange liqueur, this pie is perfect as a cool treat at a summertime fiesta!

MARGARITA PIE

makes 8 servings   hands-on time 10 min.   total time 6 hours, 30 min.

4 cups vanilla ice cream, softened
½ cup frozen limeade concentrate, softened
2 Tbsp. tequila
1 Tbsp. orange liqueur
½ tsp. lime zest

1 (9-inch) Pretzel Crust (page 246)
1 cup whipping cream
2 Tbsp. sugar
Garnishes: lime slices, coarse sea salt, chopped pretzels

1. Stir together vanilla ice cream and next 4 ingredients in a medium bowl until blended. Spoon into Pretzel Crust, spreading evenly. Cover and freeze 6 hours or until firm.

2. Let stand at room temperature 10 minutes before serving.

3. Meanwhile, beat whipping cream at high speed with an electric mixer until foamy; gradually add sugar, beating until stiff peaks form. Dollop or pipe whipped cream onto pie.

MEXICAN CHOCOLATE ICE CREAM PIE

makes 8 servings   hands-on time 30 min.
total time 10 hours, 50 min.

SPICY CINNAMON GRAHAM CRACKER CRUST

1. Preheat oven to 350°. Stir together 2½ cups cinnamon graham cracker crumbs, ½ cup melted butter, and ¼ tsp. ground red pepper; firmly press mixture on bottom and up sides of a lightly greased 9-inch pie plate.
2. Bake at 350° for 10 to 12 minutes or until lightly browned. Cool completely on a wire rack (about 30 minutes). Makes 1 (9-inch) crust.

1 (4-oz.) semisweet chocolate baking bar, finely chopped
1 (3.5-oz.) package roasted glazed pecan pieces
½ cup cinnamon graham cracker crumbs
1 pt. chocolate ice cream, softened
1 (9-inch) Spicy Cinnamon Graham Cracker Crust
1 pt. coffee ice cream, softened
1 cup whipping cream
¼ cup coffee liqueur

1. Stir together semisweet chocolate, pecan pieces, and ½ cup cinnamon graham cracker crumbs. Reserve ½ cup chocolate-pecan mixture to top pie.

2. Spread chocolate ice cream in bottom of prepared crust; top with remaining chocolate-pecan mixture. Freeze 30 minutes. Spread coffee ice cream over chocolate mixture. Cover and freeze 8 hours.

3. Beat whipping cream and coffee liqueur at medium speed with an electric mixer until stiff peaks form. Spread whipped cream mixture over pie; sprinkle with reserved ½ cup chocolate-pecan mixture. Cover and freeze 1 hour or until whipped cream is firm. Let stand 10 to 15 minutes before serving.

Just like the holiday pumpkin pie you remember, but with ice cream, this version is even better with a gingersnap crust. Make it the night before and set it out 10 minutes before dessert time!

FROSTY PUMPKIN PIE

makes 8 servings   hands-on time 10 min.
total time 8 hours, 30 min.

1 cup canned pumpkin	1 qt. vanilla ice cream, softened
½ cup firmly packed brown sugar	1 (9-inch) Gingersnap Crumb Crust
⅛ tsp. table salt	Garnishes: whipped cream, gingersnaps
1 tsp. ground cinnamon	
¼ tsp. ground nutmeg	
⅛ tsp. ground cloves	

1. Combine first 6 ingredients in a large bowl, stirring well. Fold in softened ice cream. Spoon mixture into Gingersnap Crumb Crust; cover and freeze 8 hours or overnight. Let stand at room temperature 10 minutes before serving.

GINGERSNAP CRUMB CRUST

Preheat oven to 375°. Combine 1½ cups gingersnap crumbs, ¼ cup sifted powdered sugar, and ⅓ cup melted butter, stirring well. Firmly press crumb mixture evenly over bottom and up sides of a 9-inch pie plate. Bake at 375° for 4 to 5 minutes. Makes 1 (9-inch) crust.

Since peppermint ice cream is seasonal, this recipe uses vanilla ice cream as its base for a chocolate-peppermint treat that can be made year-round.

PEPPERMINT CRUNCH ICE CREAM PIE

makes 8 servings   hands-on time 15 min.
total time 7 hours, 57 min.

4   cups vanilla ice cream, softened
¾   cup crushed hard peppermint candies (about 30 candies), divided
½   tsp. peppermint extract
5   drops red liquid food coloring (optional)
1   (9-inch) No-Bake Chocolate Wafer Crust (page 245)
1   (8-oz.) container frozen whipped topping, thawed
1   cup semisweet chocolate morsels
½   cup whipping cream

1. Stir together ice cream, ½ cup crushed peppermint candies, peppermint extract, and, if desired, food coloring in a large bowl. Spoon mixture into No-Bake Chocolate Wafer Crust, spreading evenly. Spread whipped topping over ice cream. Cover pie, and freeze 6 hours or until firm.

2. Microwave chocolate morsels and whipping cream in a small microwave-safe bowl at HIGH 1 minute or until melted, whisking until smooth and glossy. Drizzle chocolate sauce over pie, and top with remaining ¼ cup crushed peppermint candies just before serving.

the scoop • • • • • • •

To save time, substitute store-bought hot fudge topping for the home-made ganache.

STRAWBERRY-RITA PIE

makes 10 to 12 servings   hands-on time 30 min.   total time 4 hours

1 (½-gal.) container premium strawberry ice cream
1 (16-oz.) container fresh strawberries (1 qt.), stemmed
½ cup powdered sugar
1 (6-oz.) can frozen limeade concentrate, partially thawed
½ cup tequila
¼ cup orange liqueur
1 (9-inch) Pretzel Crust (page 246), baked in springform pan
Garnishes: fresh halved strawberries, fresh mint sprigs

1. Let ice cream stand at room temperature 20 minutes or until slightly softened.

2. Process strawberries and powdered sugar in food processor until pureed, stopping to scrape down sides.

3. Place ice cream in a large bowl; cut into large (3-inch) pieces. Fold strawberry mixture, limeade concentrate, tequila, and orange liqueur into ice cream until well blended. Spoon mixture into Pretzel Crust. Freeze 3 hours or until firm. Let stand 10 minutes at room temperature before serving.

note: We tested with Blue Bell Ice Cream and Triple Sec orange liqueur.

twist it up!

STRAWBERRY-LIME ICE CREAM PIE

Omit tequila and orange liqueur, and add 1 (6-oz.) can frozen orange juice concentrate, partially thawed. Proceed with recipe as directed. Let stand 15 minutes at room temperature before serving.

MOCHA-PECAN MUD PIE

makes 8 to 10 servings   hands-on time 15 min.   total time 8 hours, 35 min.

½ cup chopped pecans
Vegetable cooking spray
1   tsp. sugar
1   pt. light coffee ice cream,
     softened
1   pt. light chocolate ice cream,
     softened

1   cup coarsely chopped
     reduced-fat cream-filled
     chocolate sandwich cookies,
     divided (about 10 cookies)
1   (6-oz.) ready-made chocolate
     crumb piecrust
2   Tbsp. light chocolate syrup

1. Preheat oven to 350°. Place pecans in a single layer on a baking sheet coated with cooking spray; sprinkle evenly with sugar.

2. Bake at 350° for 8 to 10 minutes or until lightly toasted. Cool.

3. Stir together ice cream, ¾ cup cookie chunks, and ⅓ cup toasted pecans; spoon into piecrust. Freeze 10 minutes. Press remaining cookie chunks and pecans evenly on top. Cover with plastic wrap, and freeze 8 hours. Drizzle individual slices evenly with chocolate syrup.

BLACK BOTTOM CHOCOLATE MERINGUE PIE

makes 8 servings   hands-on time 30 min.   total time 7 hours

¼ cup whipping cream
1 (4-oz.) semisweet chocolate baking bar, chopped
1 (9-inch) ready-made graham cracker piecrust
4 cups chocolate ice cream, softened

4 large egg whites
⅛ tsp. table salt
¾ cup sugar
¼ cup light corn syrup

1. Bring cream to a boil in a small saucepan. Remove from heat; add chocolate. Let stand 30 seconds; whisk until smooth. Pour into bottom of piecrust. Freeze 30 minutes or until chocolate mixture is set.

2. Spoon softened ice cream into crust, spreading evenly. Cover and freeze 6 hours or until firm.

3. Preheat broiler with oven rack 8 inches from heat. Beat egg whites and salt at high speed with an electric mixer in a large bowl until soft peaks form. Meanwhile, bring sugar, corn syrup, and ¼ cup water to a boil in a medium-size heavy saucepan over medium heat; cook, without stirring, until a candy thermometer registers 238° (about 5 minutes). With mixer running at high speed, pour hot sugar syrup in a slow, steady stream over egg whites, beating until stiff peaks form.

4. Spread meringue over pie, sealing to edges. Broil 1 minute or until meringue is lightly browned. Serve immediately, or freeze until firm (about 1 hour).

the scoop · · · · · ·

Because this meringue is broiled, bake the homemade graham cracker crust in a ceramic rather than glass pie plate.

Try this pie with other fruit preserves, such as strawberry, peach, or cherry. Don't forget to garnish the finished pie with fresh fruit to match whichever preserves you choose.

BLUEBERRY STREUSEL PIE

makes 8 servings   hands-on time 10 min.   total time 7 hours

½   cup all-purpose flour
½   cup coarsely chopped pecans
⅓   cup firmly packed light brown
     sugar
3   Tbsp. butter, softened
Parchment paper

4   cups vanilla ice cream, softened
1   (9-inch) ready-made graham
     cracker piecrust
¾   cup blueberry preserves
Garnishes: fresh blueberries, fresh
     mint sprigs

1. Preheat oven to 350°. Combine first 4 ingredients in a bowl; squeeze mixture with fingertips to form clumps. Spread mixture evenly on a parchment paper-lined baking sheet. Bake at 350° for 10 minutes or until lightly browned. Cool completely (about 30 minutes).

2. Spread 2 cups softened ice cream in piecrust; dollop preserves over ice cream, and spread evenly. Spoon remaining 2 cups ice cream over preserves, spreading evenly. Sprinkle with streusel, gently pressing into ice cream. Freeze 6 hours or until firm. Let pie stand at room temperature 10 minutes before serving.

CELEBRATION-WORTHY CUPCAKES,
LAYERS, ROLLS, AND TORTES

These chocolate-cherry treats get a quick-and-easy start from a cake mix, which makes 2 dozen cupcakes. You'll have an extra dozen cupcakes to frost and enjoy, or to make another batch of this recipe.

CHOCOLATE-COVERED CHERRY ICE CREAM CUPCAKES

makes 12 cupcakes   *hands-on time 18 min.*   *total time 1 hour, 21 min.*

1 **(15.25-oz.) package devil's food cake mix**	**Vegetable cooking spray**
1¼ **cups buttermilk**	¾ **cup cherry preserves**
½ **cup vegetable oil**	3 **cups cherry-vanilla ice cream**
3 **large eggs**	¾ **cup chocolate sundae syrup**
24 **paper baking cups**	12 **fresh cherries with stems**

1. Preheat oven to 350°. Beat first 4 ingredients at low speed with an electric mixer 30 seconds. Beat at medium speed 2 minutes. Place paper baking cups in 2 (12-cup) muffin pans, and coat with cooking spray; spoon batter into cups, filling two-thirds full.

2. Bake at 350° for 18 to 20 minutes or until a wooden pick inserted in center comes out clean. Remove cupcakes from pans to wire racks, and cool completely (about 45 minutes). Reserve 12 cupcakes for another use.

3. Carefully scoop out centers of remaining 12 cupcakes, using a 1-inch melon baller and leaving a ½-inch-thick shell. Reserve centers of cupcakes for another use, if desired. Spoon cherry preserves into center of each cupcake.

4. Scoop ¼ cup ice cream onto each cupcake, and drizzle with chocolate sundae syrup. Top each cupcake with a fresh cherry. Serve immediately, or place cupcakes on a baking sheet and freeze 2 hours or until firm.

note: We tested with Breyers Cherry-Vanilla Ice Cream.

113

CAKES

TROPICAL BREEZE ICE CREAM CUPCAKES

makes 12 cupcakes   hands-on time 12 min.   total time 1 hour, 8 min.

1   (15.25-oz.) package white cake mix
⅓   cup vegetable oil
½   tsp. coconut extract
3   large egg whites
½   cup sweetened flaked coconut
24 paper baking cups

Vegetable cooking spray
3   cups pineapple-coconut ice cream
¾   cup pineapple ice-cream topping
1   (6.5-oz.) can refrigerated instant whipped cream
½   cup chopped macadamia nuts

1. Preheat oven to 350°.

2. Beat cake mix, next 3 ingredients, and 1¼ cups water at low speed with an electric mixer 30 seconds. Beat at medium speed 2 minutes. Stir in coconut. Place paper baking cups in 2 (12-cup) muffin pans, and coat with cooking spray; spoon batter into cups, filling half full.

3. Bake at 350° for 18 to 20 minutes or until a wooden pick inserted in center comes out clean. Remove from pans to wire racks, and cool completely (about 30 minutes). Reserve 12 cupcakes for another use.

4. Remove remaining 12 cupcakes from paper baking cups, and cut cupcakes in half horizontally using a serrated knife. Scoop ¼ cup ice cream onto bottom half of each cupcake; top with pineapple topping. Replace top halves of cupcakes, pressing gently. Top cupcakes evenly with instant whipped cream and chopped macadamias.

the scoop

These cupcakes can be filled with ice cream and frozen until ready to serve. Just pull them out of the freezer and top with whipped cream and macadamias.

Regular cupcakes can't hold a candle to these top-notch frozen treats. They're ideal for hot summer days when you need a cooling dose of ice cream in the afternoon.

CHOCOLATE-BRICKLE ICE CREAM CUPCAKES

makes 12 cupcakes   hands-on time 20 min.
total time 9 hours, 20 min.

1   (12-oz.) loaf pound cake
12 aluminum foil baking cups
1   (7.5-oz.) package almond brickle chips, divided
½   cup chopped toasted pecans

2   pt. chocolate mocha-fudge ice cream, softened
1   (8-oz.) container frozen whipped topping, thawed
½   (11.5-oz.) jar hot fudge sauce

1. Cut cake in half horizontally. Cut each cake half into 6 (2-inch) circles, using a 2-inch round cutter. Reserve remaining cake for another use. Place 12 foil baking cups into a 12-cup muffin pan; place 1 cake round in each cup.

2. Stir ½ cup almond brickle chips and toasted pecans into ice cream. Freeze 1 hour or until almost firm.

3. Spoon ice cream evenly over each cake round, filling to top of baking cup and mounding slightly. Dollop evenly with whipped topping. Freeze 8 hours or until firm.

4. Microwave fudge sauce at HIGH 30 seconds; drizzle over cupcakes, and sprinkle with remaining almond brickle chips just before serving.

note: We tested with HEATH Bits O'Brickle, found near the chocolate morsels in your local supermarket.

ICE CREAM SUNDAE CUPCAKES

makes 12 cupcakes   hands-on time 15 min.
total time 3 hours, 15 min.

3	cups rocky road ice cream, slightly softened	1	(7.25-oz.) bottle chocolate ice-cream shell topping
12	cream-filled chocolate sandwich cookies, crushed	¼	cup chopped dry-roasted peanuts
3	cups strawberry ice cream	1½	cups thawed whipped topping
		12	maraschino cherries with stems

1. Line 12 regular-size muffin cups with plastic wrap. Press ¼ cup rocky road ice cream in bottom of each muffin cup. Top evenly with crushed cookies. Freeze 1 hour or until firm.

2. Scoop ¼ cup strawberry ice cream in each cup on top of cookie layer. Cover; freeze 2 hours or until firm.

3. Remove plastic from ice cream cupcakes. Top each with 1 Tbsp. chocolate shell topping; let stand until set. Top each evenly with peanuts, whipped topping and cherries. Serve immediately.

the scoop • • • • • •

Place plastic wrap-lined muffin pan in freezer for 30 minutes before assembling to prevent ice cream from melting.

LEMON-BLUEBERRY ICE CREAM CUPCAKES

makes 12 cupcakes   hands-on time 15 min.   total time 8 hours, 15 min.

12 aluminum foil baking cups
24 lemon cookies, coarsely crushed
1 (21-oz.) can blueberry fruit filling
1 (14-oz.) can sweetened condensed milk
1 (6-oz.) can frozen lemonade concentrate, thawed and undiluted
1 (8-oz.) container frozen whipped topping, thawed
Crumbled lemon cookies

1. Place 12 foil baking cups into a 12-cup muffin pan; sprinkle crushed cookies evenly into cups. Spoon 2 tsp. fruit filling over cookies in each cup, reserving remaining fruit filling for another use.

2. Fold condensed milk and lemonade concentrate into whipped topping; spoon over fruit filling inprepared baking cups. Freeze 8 hours or until firm. Top with crumbled lemon cookies just before serving.

MINT-CHOCOLATE CHIP ICE CREAM CUPCAKES

makes 12 cupcakes   hands-on time 20 min.
total time 8 hours, 40 min.

1   (19.8-oz.) package fudge brownie mix
½   cup vegetable oil
3   large eggs
12   aluminum foil baking cups
½   gal. mint-chocolate chip ice cream, softened

1   (8-oz.) container frozen whipped topping, thawed
2   to 3 Tbsp. green crème de menthe (optional)
½   (4.67-oz.) package thin crème de menthe chocolate mints

1. Preheat oven to 350°. Stir together first 3 ingredients and ½ cup water until blended. Place 12 foil baking cups into a 12-cup muffin pan; spoon batter into cups.

2. Bake at 350° for 20 to 25 minutes. (A wooden pick inserted in center does not come out clean.) Cool in pans on wire racks 10 minutes; remove from pans, keeping baking cups on cupcakes. Cool completely on wire racks.

3. Return cooled cupcakes to muffin pans, and spoon ice cream evenly over each. Freeze 8 hours or until firm.

4. Stir together whipped topping and, if desired, liqueur. Dollop evenly over ice cream. Freeze until ready to serve.

5. Pull a vegetable peeler down sides of mints, making tiny curls; sprinkle curls over cupcakes just before serving.

note: We tested with Andes Crème De Menthe Thins.

GERMAN CHOCOLATE ICE CREAM CUPCAKES

makes 12 cupcakes   hands-on time 21 min.   total time 2 hours, 46 min.

1½   cups sweetened flaked coconut
1   cup chopped toasted pecans
3½   cups vanilla ice cream, softened
1   (15.25-oz.) package German chocolate cake mix
1¼   cups milk
½   cup butter, melted
3   large eggs

1   (4-oz.) German chocolate baking bar, chopped
24   paper baking cups
Vegetable cooking spray
1   cup ready-to-spread coconut-pecan frosting
12   toasted chopped pecans

1. Preheat oven to 350°. Place coconut in a single layer in a shallow baking pan. Bake at 350° for 8 to 10 minutes or until toasted, stirring occasionally. Cool completely (about 15 minutes).

2. Fold coconut and chopped toasted pecans into vanilla ice cream. Freeze 2 hours or until firm.

3. Meanwhile, beat cake mix and next 3 ingredients at low speed with an electric mixer 30 seconds. Beat at medium speed 2 minutes. Microwave chopped chocolate in a small microwave-safe bowl at HIGH 1 to 1½ minutes or until melted and smooth, stirring at 30-second intervals. Stir into batter. Place paper baking cups in 2 (12-cup) muffin pans, and coat with cooking spray; spoon batter into cups, filling three-fourths full.

4. Bake at 350° for 18 to 20 minutes or until a wooden pick inserted in center comes out clean. Remove from pans to wire racks, and cool completely (about 30 minutes). Reserve 12 cupcakes for another use.

5. Carefully scoop out centers of remaining 12 cupcakes, using a 1-inch melon baller and leaving a ½-inch-thick shell. Reserve centers of cupcakes for another use, if desired. Spoon frosting into center of each cupcake.

6. Scoop ⅓ cup ice cream onto each cupcake, and top each with toasted chopped pecans. Serve immediately, or place cupcakes on a baking sheet and freeze 2 hours or until firm.

We've taken everyone's favorite cheesecake and turned it into ice cream-packed cupcakes! These would be perfect for Valentine's Day or for any pink-themed party.

STRAWBERRY CHEESECAKE ICE CREAM CUPCAKES

*makes 12 cupcakes   hands-on time 18 min.
total time 3 hours, 58 min.*

¾ cup graham cracker crumbs
1   Tbsp. granulated sugar
2   Tbsp. butter, melted
12 paper baking cups
1   (8-oz.) package cream cheese, softened

⅓ cup powdered sugar
½ tsp. lemon zest
1½ cups thawed whipped topping
4   cups strawberry ice cream
6   fresh strawberries, halved

1. Preheat oven to 350°. Stir together first 3 ingredients in a small bowl. Place paper baking cups in a 12-cup muffin pan; spoon crumb mixture into cups, pressing into bottoms of cups.

the scoop

We liked the cookie cups soft, but for a crispier cookie, increase the bake time.

2. Bake at 350° for 8 to 10 minutes or until golden brown. Cool completely on a wire rack (about 30 minutes).

3. Beat cream cheese, powdered sugar, and lemon zest at medium speed with an electric mixer until creamy. Fold in whipped topping. Divide cream cheese mixture evenly among muffin cups. Freeze 1 hour.

4. Scoop ⅓ cup strawberry ice cream into each muffin cup. Freeze 2 hours or until firm.

5. Top each cupcake with a strawberry half just before serving.

STRAWBERRIES-AND-CREAM CAKE ROLL

makes 10 servings   hands-on time 28 min.
total time 7 hours, 43 min.

Vegetable cooking spray
Parchment paper
4   large eggs, separated
1   cup granulated sugar, divided
¾   cup all-purpose flour
1   tsp. baking powder
½   tsp. table salt

2   tsp. vanilla extract, divided
¼   cup powdered sugar
4   cups strawberry ice cream, softened
¾   cup whipping cream
1   Tbsp. powdered sugar
1   cup sliced fresh strawberries

1. Preheat oven to 375°. Coat a 15- x 10-inch jelly-roll pan with cooking spray; line bottom of pan with parchment paper.

2. Beat egg whites at high speed with an electric mixer in a medium bowl until foamy. Gradually add ½ cup granulated sugar, 1 Tbsp. at a time, beating until stiff peaks form and sugar dissolves (about 2 to 4 minutes).

3. Stir together flour, baking powder, and salt in a small bowl. Beat egg yolks and remaining ½ cup granulated sugar at high speed with an electric mixer in a large bowl 1 minute or until thick and pale. Add 1 tsp. vanilla; beat until blended. Fold in one-fourth of egg white mixture; fold in remaining egg white mixture. Fold in flour mixture just until blended; spread batter evenly in prepared pan.

4. Bake at 375° for 14 minutes or until cake springs back when lightly touched.

5. Meanwhile, sift ¼ cup powdered sugar over a smooth kitchen towel. Loosen edges of cake from pan with a knife; invert cake onto prepared towel. Carefully remove parchment paper, and discard. Starting at 1 long side, roll up cake and towel together. Cool completely (about 1 hour).

6. Unroll cake. Spread strawberry ice cream over cake, leaving a 1-inch border; roll up, jelly-roll fashion, ending seam side down. Wrap cake in plastic wrap, sealing at both ends. Freeze 6 hours or until firm.

7. Let stand at room temperature 10 minutes before serving. Beat whipping cream until foamy; add 1 Tbsp. powdered sugar and remaining 1 tsp. vanilla, beating until stiff peaks form. Top each slice of cake with whipped cream and fresh strawberries.

BROWNIE BAKED ALASKA

makes 10 to 12 servings   hands-on time 30 min.
total time 2 hours, 5 min.

1	qt. vanilla ice cream, softened	½	tsp. baking powder
½	cup butter, softened	2	Tbsp. unsweetened cocoa
2	cups sugar, divided	¼	tsp. table salt
2	large eggs	1	tsp. vanilla extract
1	cup all-purpose flour	5	pasteurized egg whites

1. Line a 1-qt. bowl (about 7 inches in diameter) with plastic wrap, allowing 2 to 3 inches to extend over sides. Pack ice cream into bowl, and freeze until very firm.

2. Preheat oven to 350°. Beat butter and 1 cup sugar at medium speed with an electric mixer until light and fluffy. Add eggs, 1 at a time, beating well after each addition. Combine flour and next 3 ingredients in a small bowl; add to butter mixture, blending well. Stir in vanilla.

3. Spoon batter into a greased and floured 8-inch round cake pan. Bake at 350° for 25 to 30 minutes or until a wooden pick inserted in center comes out clean. Cool in pan 10 minutes; remove to a wire rack. Cool completely (about 1 hour).

4. Increase oven temperature to 500°. Place brownie layer on an ovenproof serving dish. Invert bowl of ice cream onto brownie layer; remove bowl, leaving plastic wrap on ice cream. Place cake in freezer.

5. Beat egg whites at medium speed with an electric mixer until foamy; gradually beat in remaining 1 cup sugar, 1 Tbsp. at a time, beating until stiff peaks form and sugar dissolves. Remove cake from freezer. Remove and discard plastic wrap. Spread meringue over surface, sealing edges.

6. Bake at 500° for 2 to 3 minutes or until meringue peaks are lightly browned. Serve immediately.

the scoop

After the meringue is sealed, the dessert can be returned to the freezer for up to 1 week and baked just before serving.

CAKES

KEY LIME PIE ICE CREAM CAKE ROLLS

makes 2 cake rolls (10 to 12 servings each)   hands-on time 20 min.
total time 9 hours, 5 min.

Parchment paper
1 (16-oz.) package angel food cake mix
⅔ cup powdered sugar
1 cup coarsely crumbled graham crackers (4 sheets)
5 Tbsp. Key lime juice

1 tsp. grated lime zest
½ gal. vanilla ice cream, softened
1 (16-oz.) container frozen whipped topping, thawed
Garnishes: grated lime zest, lime slices, fresh mint sprigs

1. Preheat oven to 325°. Line 2 (15- x 10-inch) jelly-roll pans with parchment or wax paper. Prepare angel food cake mix batter according to package directions. Pour evenly into prepared pans.

2. Bake at 325° for 15 to 20 minutes or until a wooden pick inserted in center comes out clean. Cool in pans on wire racks 10 minutes. (If baking cakes in 1 oven, bake on middle 2 racks for 10 minutes; then switch places, and continue baking for 5 to 10 minutes.)

3. Sift ⅓ cup powdered sugar evenly over each of 2 (24- x 18-inch) pieces heavy-duty aluminum foil.

4. Loosen edges of cakes from pans. Invert each slightly warm cake onto a prepared foil piece. Carefully remove parchment paper, and discard. Place a cloth towel on top of each cake. Starting at 1 long side, roll up foil, cake, and towel together. Chill rolled cakes 30 minutes or until completely cool. Unroll and remove towels. (Keep each cake on foil piece.)

5. Stir crumbled graham crackers, Key lime juice, and 1 tsp. grated lime zest into softened ice cream. Spread half of ice cream over top of 1 prepared cake on foil piece, leaving a 1-inch border, and roll up jelly-roll fashion, ending seam side down. Wrap cake roll with foil piece, sealing at both ends. Place in freezer. Repeat procedure with remaining ice cream and prepared cake on foil piece.

6. Freeze cake rolls at least 8 hours or until firm. Unwrap and frost each evenly with whipped topping. Serve immediately, or freeze cake roll 1 hour or until whipped topping is firm; rewrap with foil, and freeze until ready to serve.

HOT FUDGE SUNDAE CAKE ROLLS

makes 2 cake rolls (10 to 12 servings each)   hands-on time 40 min.
total time 9 hours, 40 min.

Parchment paper
1   (16-oz.) package angel food
    cake mix
¼   cup unsweetened cocoa
⅔   cup powdered sugar
½   gal. vanilla ice cream, softened
1   (10-oz.) jar maraschino cherries,
    drained and chopped

1   (16-oz.) container frozen whipped
    topping, thawed
Hot Fudge Ice Cream Topping
    (page 232)
Garnishes: grated chocolate,
    maraschino cherries

1. Preheat oven to 325°. Line 2 (15- x 10-inch) jelly-roll pans with parchment or
wax paper. Prepare angel food cake mix batter according to package directions,
adding unsweetened cocoa. Pour evenly into prepared pans.

2. Bake at 325° for 15 to 20 minutes or until a wooden pick inserted in center
comes out clean. Cool in pans on wire racks 10 minutes. (If baking cakes in
1 oven, bake on middle 2 racks for 10 minutes; then switch places, and continue
baking for 5 to 10 minutes.)

3. Sift ⅔ cup powdered sugar evenly over 2 (24- x 18-inch) pieces heavy-duty
aluminum foil. Loosen edges of cakes from pans. Invert each slightly warm cake
onto a prepared foil piece. Carefully remove parchment paper, and discard.
Place a cloth towel on top of each cake. Starting at 1 long side, roll up foil, cake,
and towel together.

4. Chill rolled cakes 30 minutes or until completely cool. Unroll cakes, and
remove towels. (Keep each cake on foil piece.) Spread half of ice cream over
top of 1 prepared cake on foil piece, leaving a 1-inch border; sprinkle with half of
chopped cherries, and roll up, jelly-roll fashion, ending seam side down. Wrap
cake roll with foil piece, sealing at both ends. Place in freezer. Repeat procedure
with remaining ice cream, cherries, and prepared cake on foil piece.

5. Freeze cake rolls at least 8 hours or until firm. Unwrap and frost each evenly
with whipped topping. Serve with Hot Fudge Ice Cream Topping.

MINT-CHOCOLATE CHIP ICE CREAM CAKE

makes 10 to 12 servings   hands-on time 30 min.
total time 10 hours, 30 min., including ganache

CHOCOLATE GANACHE

1. Microwave 1 (4-oz.) semisweet chocolate baking bar, chopped, and 4 Tbsp. whipping cream in a microwave-safe bowl at HIGH 1 minute or until melted, stirring at 30-second intervals. Stir in up to 4 Tbsp. additional cream for desired consistency. Use immediately. Makes about 1 cup.

Parchment paper
½ cup butter, softened
¾ cup sugar
1 large egg
1 tsp. vanilla extract
1 cup all-purpose flour
⅓ cup unsweetened cocoa
1 tsp. baking soda
¾ cup hot strong brewed coffee

1 tsp. white vinegar
½ gal. mint-chocolate chip ice cream, softened
10 chocolate wafers, coarsely crushed
Chocolate Ganache
Garnishes: sweetened whipped cream, thin crème de menthe chocolate mints

1. Preheat oven to 350°. Grease and flour 3 (8-inch) round cake pans. Line with parchment paper.

2. Beat butter and sugar at medium speed with a heavy-duty electric stand mixer until creamy. Add egg, beating just until blended. Beat in vanilla. Combine flour, cocoa, and baking soda. Add to butter mixture alternately with coffee, beating until blended. Stir in vinegar. Spoon into pans.

3. Bake at 350° for 12 to 14 minutes or until a wooden pick inserted in center comes out clean. Cool in pans on a wire rack 10 minutes. Remove from pans to wire racks, discard parchment paper, and cool completely (about 1 hour).

4. Place 1 cake layer in a 9-inch springform pan. Top with one-third of ice cream (about 2⅓ cups); sprinkle with half of crushed wafers. Repeat layers once. Top with remaining cake layer and ice cream. Freeze 8 to 12 hours.

5. Remove cake from springform pan, and place on a cake stand or plate. Spread ganache over top of cake. Let stand 15 minutes before serving.

STRAWBERRY SEMIFREDDO SHORTCAKE

makes 16 servings   hands-on time 30 min.
total time 5 hours, 45 min.

2   (3-oz.) packages soft ladyfingers
2   pt. strawberry ice cream, softened
1   pt. strawberry sorbet, softened
1   pt. fresh strawberries, hulled
2   Tbsp. powdered sugar
½   (7-oz.) jar marshmallow crème
1   cup heavy cream

1. Arrange ladyfingers around sides and on bottom of a 9-inch springform pan. (Reserve any remaining ladyfingers for another use.) Spread strawberry ice cream over ladyfingers, and freeze 30 minutes.

2. Spread softened strawberry sorbet over ice cream. Freeze 30 minutes.

3. Process strawberries and powdered sugar in a food processor 1 minute or until pureed. Reserve ¼ cup mixture. Whisk remaining strawberry mixture into marshmallow crème until well blended.

4. Beat cream at high speed with an electric mixer until stiff peaks form. Fold into marshmallow mixture. Pour over sorbet in pan. Drizzle reserved strawberry mixture over top, and gently swirl with a paring knife. Freeze 4 hours or until firm. Let ice-cream cake stand at room temperature 15 minutes before serving.

note: We tested with Blue Bell Strawberry Ice Cream and Häagen-Dazs Strawberry Sorbet.

the scoop · · · · · · · ·

Look for packages of soft ladyfingers in the bakery section of the grocery store.

EASY MOCHA CHIP ICE CREAM CAKE

makes 8 to 10 servings   hands-on time 32 min.
total time 5 hours, 15 min., including ganache

MOCHA GANACHE

1. Microwave 1 (4-oz.) semisweet chocolate baking bar, chopped; 1 tsp. instant espresso; and 3 Tbsp. whipping cream in a microwave-safe bowl at HIGH 1 minute or until melted and smooth, stirring at 30-second intervals. Whisk in additional 1 Tbsp. cream until smooth. Use immediately. Makes about ¾ cup.

1 pt. premium dark chocolate chunk-coffee ice cream, softened
3 sugar cones, crushed
⅓ cup chocolate fudge ice-cream shell topping
1 (14-oz.) container premium chocolate-chocolate chip ice cream, softened
6 cream-filled chocolate sandwich cookies, finely crushed
Mocha Ganache
Garnish: candy-and-chocolate-covered coffee beans

1. Line an 8- x 5-inch loaf pan with plastic wrap, allowing 3 inches to extend over sides. Spread chocolate chunk-coffee ice cream in pan. Sprinkle with crushed cones, and drizzle with shell topping. Freeze 30 minutes.

2. Spread chocolate-chocolate chip ice cream over topping. Top with crushed cookies, pressing into ice cream. Freeze 4 hours or until firm.

3. Lift ice cream loaf from pan, using plastic wrap as handles; invert onto a serving plate. Discard plastic wrap. Slowly pour ganache over ice cream loaf, allowing ganache to drip down sides. Freeze 10 minutes. Let stand at room temperature 10 minutes before serving.

Homemade cake layers make this impressive frozen dessert especially delicious, but if you're in a pinch, you can substitute a red velvet cake mix.

RED VELVET ICE CREAM CAKE

makes 20 servings   hands-on time 27 min.
total time 7 hours, 2 min.

2½ cups all-purpose flour
1½ cups sugar
1   Tbsp. unsweetened cocoa
1   tsp. baking soda
1   tsp. table salt
1   cup vegetable oil
1   cup buttermilk
1   tsp. cider vinegar
1   tsp. vanilla extract

2   large eggs
1   (1-oz.) bottle red liquid food coloring
2   (8-oz.) packages cream cheese, softened
½   gal. container vanilla ice cream
1   (12-oz.) container frozen whipped topping, thawed
Garnish: chocolate curls

1. Preheat oven to 350°. Whisk together first 5 ingredients in a large bowl until well blended. Whisk together oil and next 5 ingredients; add to flour mixture, whisking until blended. Pour batter into 2 greased and floured 9-inch round cake pans.

2. Bake at 350° for 25 minutes or until a wooden pick inserted in center comes out clean. Cool in pans on wire racks 10 minutes; remove from pans to wire racks, and cool completely (about 1 hour). Cut each cake layer in half horizontally, using a serrated knife. Wrap cake layers in plastic wrap.

3. Line 3 (9-inch) round cake pans with 2 layers of plastic wrap, allowing 3 inches to extend over sides. Beat cream cheese at high speed with a heavy-duty electric stand mixer, using whisk attachment until smooth. Gradually add ice cream, ½ cup at a time, beating until blended. Divide ice cream mixture evenly among prepared pans, spreading evenly. Wrap with plastic wrap overhang; freeze 4 hours or until firm.

4. Place 1 cake layer, cut side up, on a serving plate; top with 1 ice cream layer. Repeat layers twice. Top with remaining cake layer, cut side down. Spread whipped topping on top and sides of cake. Freeze at least 1 hour before serving.

CAKES

TRES LECHES ICE CREAM CAKE

makes 12 servings   hands-on time 27 min.
total time 9 hours, 59 min.

1   (15.25-oz.) package vanilla
    cake mix
1   cup evaporated milk
½   cup vegetable oil
3   large eggs
1   (14-oz.) can sweetened
    condensed milk, divided

¾   cup jarred butterscotch-caramel
    topping
3   cups vanilla ice cream, softened
1½ cups heavy cream
1   tsp. vanilla extract

1. Preheat oven to 350°. Beat first 4 ingredients at low speed with an electric mixer 30 seconds. Beat at medium speed 2 minutes. Pour batter into 2 greased and floured 9-inch round cake pans.

2. Bake at 350° for 20 to 22 minutes or until a wooden pick inserted in center comes out clean. Cool in pans on wire racks 10 minutes; remove from pans to wire racks. While cake layers are warm, level off domed portion of cake with a serrated knife.

3. Stir together ¾ cup sweetened condensed milk and butterscotch-caramel topping in a small bowl. Spoon ½ cup caramel mixture over each warm cake layer, spreading with an offset spatula to soak into cake. Cool completely (about 1 hour). Cover and refrigerate remaining ½ cup caramel mixture.

4. Line a 9-inch springform pan with 2 layers of plastic wrap, allowing 3 inches to extend over sides. Place 1 cake layer, caramel side up, in bottom of pan. Spread ice cream evenly over cake. Top with remaining cake layer, caramel side down. Wrap with plastic overhang; freeze 8 hours or until firm.

5. Beat remaining ½ cup sweetened condensed milk, cream, and vanilla at high speed with an electric mixer until stiff peaks form. Lift cake from springform pan, using plastic wrap as handles. Unwrap cake, and place on a serving plate. Spread whipped cream mixture on top and sides of cake.

6. Heat remaining ½ cup chilled caramel mixture in a small microwave-safe bowl at HIGH 30 seconds to 1 minute or until warm. Spoon warm caramel mixture over cake slices; serve immediately.

note: We tested with Mrs. Richardson's Butterscotch-Caramel Topping.

Elegant yet fun, this make-ahead dessert is perfect for a dinner party. Dark chocolate, ricotta, pistachios, and sugar cone pieces make this torte taste just like a cannoli.

CANNOLI ICE CREAM TORTE

makes 10 servings   hands-on time 10 min.
total time 5 hours, 15 min.

½   cup sugar
1   (15-oz.) container ricotta cheese
1   cup milk
1   Tbsp. lemon zest
½   tsp. vanilla extract
1   cup dark chocolate morsels, chopped

1   cup chopped pistachios
6   sugar cones, crushed (1 cup)
½   cup semisweet chocolate mini-morsels
½   cup chocolate syrup

1. Bring sugar and ½ cup water to a boil in a medium saucepan over medium-high heat. Boil, stirring occasionally, 4 to 5 minutes or until sugar is dissolved and mixture is clear. Pour into a large bowl; let cool 30 to 40 minutes or to room temperature.

2. Add ricotta cheese, milk, lemon zest, and vanilla to sugar syrup in bowl, whisking until well blended.

3. Pour mixture into freezer container of a 1½-qt. electric ice cream maker, and freeze according to manufacturer's instructions. (Instructions and times may vary.)

4. Stir together dark chocolate morsels, pistachios, and crushed cones; fold into ice cream.

5. Line a 9- x 5-inch loaf pan with plastic wrap, allowing 2 to 3 inches to extend over sides. Place mini-morsels in bottom of pan; pour ice cream over mini-morsels. Cover and freeze at least 4 hours or until firm.

6. Lift torte from pan, using plastic wrap sides as handles. Let stand 5 minutes before serving. Cut into 10 slices; drizzle slices with chocolate syrup.

TIRAMISÙ ICE CREAM CAKE

makes 10 to 12 servings   hands-on time 16 min.
total time 9 hours, 56 min.

20 chocolate wafers, finely crushed (1 cup)
1   cup plus 3 Tbsp. sugar, divided
3   Tbsp. butter, melted
1⅓ cups strong brewed coffee
1   cup heavy cream
2   Tbsp. coffee liqueur
1   (8-oz.) package mascarpone cheese
3   (3-oz.) packages ladyfingers
6   cups coffee ice cream, softened
1   Tbsp. unsweetened cocoa

1. Preheat oven to 350°. Stir together chocolate wafer crumbs, 3 Tbsp. sugar, and melted butter in a small bowl; press mixture onto bottom of a 10-inch springform pan.

2. Bake at 350° for 10 minutes. Cool on a wire rack (about 30 minutes).

3. Meanwhile, bring coffee and ¾ cup sugar to a boil in a small saucepan over medium-high heat, stirring until sugar is dissolved. Remove from heat, and cool completely (about 30 minutes).

4. Beat heavy cream, coffee liqueur, mascarpone cheese, and remaining ¼ cup sugar at medium speed with an electric mixer until soft peaks form.

5. Stand ladyfingers around edge of prepared pan; brush lightly with ¼ cup coffee syrup. Spread 3 cups ice cream over crust; top with a layer of ladyfingers, and brush with ¾ cup coffee syrup. Spread mascarpone cheese mixture over ladyfinger layer; top with another layer of ladyfingers, and brush with remaining ¾ cup coffee syrup. Spread remaining 3 cups ice cream over ladyfinger layer; dust with cocoa. Cover and freeze 8 to 24 hours. Remove sides of pan. Let stand 10 minutes before serving.

the scoop · · · · · · ·

Be sure not to overbeat the whipping cream-mascarpone cheese mixture, as it may curdle.

Layered with fudgy brownies and chock-full of nuts, marshmallows, and fudge topping, this ice cream cake is a chocolate lover's dream. It would make the perfect ice cream birthday cake.

ROCKY ROAD ICE CREAM CAKE

makes 10 servings   hands-on time 15 min.
total time 9 hours, 33 min.

1   (18.75-oz.) premium brownie mix
⅓   cup vegetable oil
1   large egg
1   cup miniature marshmallows
1   cup walnuts halves, chopped
½   cup semisweet chocolate mini-morsels

½   cup hot fudge topping
4   cups rocky road ice cream, softened
Garnishes: chopped walnuts, miniature marshmallows, and semisweet chocolate mini-morsels

1. Preheat oven to 325°. Line bottom and sides of a 13- x 9-inch pan with aluminum foil, allowing 2 to 3 inches to extend over 2 long sides of pan; lightly grease foil.

2. Stir together first 3 ingredients and ¼ cup water in a medium bowl; spread batter in prepared pan.

3. Bake at 325° for 15 to 18 minutes or until a wooden pick inserted in center comes out with a few moist crumbs. Cool completely in pan on a wire rack (about 1 hour). Lift brownies from pan, using foil sides as handles. Cut crosswise into thirds; carefully remove foil.

4. Line bottom and sides of a 9- x 5-inch loaf pan with 2 layers of plastic wrap, allowing 3 inches to extend over all sides. Stir together marshmallows, walnuts, and mini-morsels in a medium bowl. Spoon fudge topping into a zip-top plastic freezer bag. Snip 1 corner of bag to make a hole (about ¼ inch in diameter).

5. Place one-third of brownie in bottom of prepared loaf pan. Sprinkle with half of marshmallow mixture; drizzle with half of fudge topping. Dollop with half of softened ice cream, spreading gently. Repeat layers once. Top with remaining one-third of brownie. Wrap with plastic overhang; freeze 8 hours or until firm.

6. Lift cake from pan, using plastic wrap as handles. Unwrap cake, and cut crosswise into 10 slices.

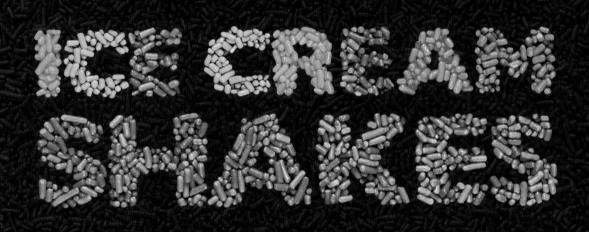

SIPPABLE, FROSTY, SWIRLED DELIGHTS

Sip this spin on the original peach Melba dessert created for Australian opera singer Dame Nellie Melba, which consisted of a poached peach half topped with ice cream, raspberries, and almonds.

PEACH MELBA SHAKE

makes 4 servings   hands-on time 10 min.   total time 10 min.

2   cups peeled, sliced fresh peaches (about 2 medium-size ripe peaches)
2   cups vanilla ice cream
¾   cup milk
3   Tbsp. sugar
¼   tsp. almond extract
½   cup fresh raspberries
½   cup sugar
Garnishes: fresh peach slices, raspberries, mint sprigs

1. Process first 5 ingredients in a food processor or blender until smooth, stopping to scrape down sides as needed. Pour into glasses.

2. Process raspberries and ½ cup sugar until smooth; swirl evenly into shakes. Serve immediately.

the scoop . . . .

If you prefer a different berry flavor, substitute ½ cup fresh strawberries for the raspberries.

149

SHAKES

LEMON-BLUEBERRY CHEESECAKE SHAKE

makes 4 servings   hands-on time 10 min.   total time 10 min.

1   (3-oz.) package cream cheese
1   pt. vanilla ice cream
1   cup fresh or frozen blueberries
½   cup milk
¼   cup sugar
2   tsp. grated lemon zest
1   tsp. vanilla extract
Garnish: grated lemon zest

1. Microwave cream cheese in a small microwave-safe bowl at HIGH 30 seconds; stir until smooth.

2. Process melted cream cheese, ice cream, blueberries, and remaining ingredients in a blender until smooth, stopping to scrape down sides as needed. Pour into glasses. Serve immediately.

HONEY-DATE SHAKE

makes 3 servings   hands-on time 5 min.   total time 5 min.

1   cup milk
12   pitted Medjool dates, coarsely
     chopped (1 cup)

2   tsp. vanilla extract
4   cups vanilla ice cream
¼   cup honey

1. Process first 3 ingredients in a blender until smooth, stopping to scrape down sides as needed. Add ice cream and honey; process until smooth. Pour into glasses. Serve immediately.

the scoop • • • • • • •

For an adult version of this sweet Middle Eastern-inspired shake, add 2 Tbsp. amaretto liqueur.

DOUBLE IRISH CREAM

makes 3 servings   *hands-on time 5 min.*
total time 5 min.

½ cup Irish cream liqueur
2½ cups vanilla ice cream
¼ cup Irish whiskey

Garnishes: sweetened whipped cream, freshly grated nutmeg

1. Process all ingredients in a blender until smooth, stopping to scrape down sides as needed. Pour into glasses. Serve immediately.

Take a frozen prepared cheesecake and turn it into a rich and creamy milkshake packed with fresh strawberries and graham crackers. Whip these up for movie night or a summertime dessert.

STRAWBERRY CHEESECAKE MILKSHAKES

makes 4 servings   hands-on time 15 min.   total time 15 min.

3   cups vanilla ice cream
1½ cups sliced fresh strawberries
1   cup milk
2   Tbsp. strawberry syrup
2   tsp. vanilla extract
1   slice frozen cheesecake (from 5.6-oz. box), chopped

1   cup refrigerated instant whipped cream
1   to 2 graham cracker squares, crushed
Garnish: whole strawberries

1. Process ice cream, sliced strawberries, milk, strawberry syrup, vanilla, and chopped cheesecake in a blender about 1 minute until smooth, stopping to scrape down sides as needed. (Blender will be full; blend in 2 batches, if necessary.)

2. Pour evenly into 4 glasses. Top each shake with whipped cream; sprinkle with cracker crumbs. Serve immediately.

the scoop . . . .

If fresh strawberries are not in season, substitute frozen unsweetened whole ones. You may need to add more milk, because the frozen fruit will deliver a thicker consistency.

This strawberries-and-ice cream shake gets a grown-up kick from amaretto liqueur. Serve it up in champagne coupes for a fancy look.

STRAWBERRY-AMARETTO MILKSHAKE

makes 4 servings   hands-on time 10 min.   total time 30 min.

2   cups sliced fresh strawberries
½   cup amaretto liqueur
2   Tbsp. sugar

2   cups vanilla ice cream
Garnishes: sweetened whipped cream, chopped fresh strawberries

1. Stir together sliced fresh strawberries, amaretto liqueur, and 2 Tbsp. sugar; let stand 20 minutes.

2. Process strawberry mixture and ice cream in a blender until smooth, stopping to scrape down sides as needed. Pour into glasses. Serve immediately.

VERY STRAWBERRY MILKSHAKES

makes 4 servings   hands-on time 5 min.   total time 5 min.

1   pt. fresh strawberry halves, frozen
¾   cup milk
¼   cup powdered sugar
½   tsp. vanilla extract

1   pt. strawberry ice cream
Garnishes: sweetened whipped cream,
     sliced strawberries

1. Process first 4 ingredients in a blender until smooth, stopping to scrape down sides as needed. Add ice cream, and process until blended. Pour into glasses. Serve immediately.

the scoop • • • • • • •

Serve these classic strawberry shakes in chilled tall glasses with pink straws for a real sodashop feel.

For a chocolatey fix, look no further than an icy glass of this decadent shake. Don't forget to top it off with loads of marshmallows, whipped cream, and chocolate syrup!

MISSISSIPPI MUDSLIDES

makes 4 servings   hands-on time 5 min.   total time 5 min.

1   pt. chocolate ice cream
1   pt. coffee ice cream
1   cup milk

½   cup bourbon
Garnishes: whipped cream, chocolate
      syrup, marshmallows

1. Process first 4 ingredients in a blender until smooth, stopping to scrape down sides as needed. Pour into glasses. Serve immediately.

the scoop • • • • • • •

For a non-alcoholic version of this shake, just omit the bourbon and increase the milk to 1½ cups.

Fill tall glasses with a shake made from everything that makes a sundae so delicious: vanilla ice cream, hot fudge, caramel syrup, whipped cream, brownies, and cherries.

HOT FUDGE SUNDAE SHAKE

makes 4 servings   hands-on time 10 min.   total time 10 min.

1	pt. vanilla bean ice cream
½	cup milk
8	Tbsp. hot fudge topping, warmed
8	Tbsp. caramel topping, warmed

1	(8.5-oz.) can refrigerated instant whipped cream
¼	cup crumbled brownies, divided
4	maraschino cherries with stems

1. Process ice cream and milk in a blender until smooth, stopping to scrape down sides as needed.

2. Divide half of ice cream mixture evenly among 4 (8-oz.) glasses. Top each with 1 Tbsp. fudge topping and 1 Tbsp. caramel topping. Repeat layers with remaining ice cream mixture and fudge and caramel toppings.

3. Top each with whipped cream; sprinkle with 1 Tbsp. crumbled brownies, and top with a cherry. Serve immediately.

note: We tested with Häagen-Dazs Vanilla Bean Ice Cream and Smucker's Hot Fudge and Caramel Flavored Toppings.

the scoop . . . .

This recipe is a great way to use leftover brownies, or you can use prepared brownies from the bakery section of your supermarket.

BLACKBERRY COBBLER MILKSHAKES

makes 4 servings   hands-on time 10 min.   total time 20 min.

½ (14.1-oz.) package refrigerated
    piecrusts
2   Tbsp. butter, melted
2   Tbsp. turbinado sugar (raw sugar)
    or granulated sugar
½   tsp. ground cinnamon

4   cups vanilla ice cream
½   cup milk
2   cups fresh or frozen (do not thaw)
    blackberries
Garnish: additional blackberries

1. Preheat oven to 450°. Unroll piecrust, and cut into 4 (4-inch) triangles. Place triangles and trimmings on ungreased baking sheet. Brush with melted butter. Sprinkle with sugar and cinnamon.

2. Bake at 450° for 8 to 9 minutes or until golden brown. Cool completely on a wire rack.

3. Process 2 cups ice cream, ¼ cup milk, and 1 cup blackberries in a blender about 1 minute or until smooth, stopping to scrap down sides as needed. Pour into 2 glasses. Repeat with remaining 2 cups ice cream, ¼ cup milk, and 1 cup blackberries.

4. Top each shake with 1 piecrust triangle. Serve immediately.

These tropical shakes are guaranteed to delight and will make you feel like you're on vacation. If there's a perfect milkshake for breakfast, we'd pick this one!

COCONUT-ORANGE DELIGHT SHAKE

makes 4 servings   hands-on time 10 min.   total time 10 min.

1   pt. vanilla ice cream
½   cup cream of coconut
½   cup milk
2   Tbsp. thawed orange juice
     concentrate

1½   tsp. grated orange zest
Garnishes: grated orange or lemon
     zest, fresh mint leaves

1. Process all ingredients in a blender until smooth, stopping to scrape down sides as needed. Pour into glasses. Serve immediately.

note: We tested with Coco López Cream of Coconut.

the scoop ·······

Transform this shake into more of a cocktail by decreasing the milk to ¼ cup and adding ¼ cup rum.

Make this shake as a pick-me-up on a busy day or as a rich breakfast treat. It tastes just like a coffeeshop frozen cappuccino drink!

"MAKE MY AFTERNOON" MOCHA

makes 4 servings   hands-on time 5 min.   total time 5 min.

2   cups chocolate milk
2   cups vanilla or chocolate ice cream
1   cup ice cubes

2   Tbsp. chocolate syrup
2   packets instant iced coffee granules (from a 5.6-oz. box)

1. Process all ingredients in a blender until ice is crushed and mixture is smooth, stopping to scrape down sides as needed. Pour into glasses. Serve immediately.

note: We tested with Starbucks Via Ready Brew Iced Coffee Packets.

MOCHA-MINT SHAKE

makes 4 servings   hands-on time 5 min.   total time 5 min.

4   cups vanilla ice cream
1½   cups milk
½   cup peppermint schnapps or
     ¼ tsp. peppermint extract

1   Tbsp. instant coffee granules
2   Tbsp. chocolate syrup

1. Process all ingredients in a blender until smooth, stopping to scrape down sides as needed. Pour into glasses. Serve immediately.

BANANA-MOCHA SHAKE

makes 4 servings   hands-on time 5 min.   total time 5 min.

3   medium-size ripe bananas
2   cups coffee ice cream
1   cup milk
¼   cup chocolate syrup

Garnishes: sweetened whipped cream,
    chopped chocolate-covered
    espresso beans

1. Process all ingredients in a blender 1 minute or until smooth, stopping to scrape down sides as needed. Pour into glasses. Serve immediately.

PINEAPPLE-BUTTERMILK SHAKE

makes 6 servings   hands-on time 5 min.   total time 5 min.

1   (8-oz.) can unsweetened
    pineapple chunks, drained and
    frozen

1   qt. vanilla ice cream
½   cup firmly packed brown sugar
2   cups buttermilk

1. Process all ingredients in a blender until smooth, stopping to scrape down sides as needed. Pour into glasses. Serve immediately.

twist it up!

LIGHT PINEAPPLE-BUTTERMILK SHAKE

Substitute low-fat vanilla ice cream and fat-free buttermilk; reduce brown sugar to ⅓ cup. Proceed with recipe as directed, and serve immediately.

Egg creams are a classic Brooklyn soda fountain concoction, likely named for the foamy, egg white–like head that tops the drink. This version adds ice cream to make it a float.

EGG CREAM FLOATS

makes 4 servings   hands-on time 5 min.   total time 5 min.

½ cup chocolate syrup
2 cups milk
2 cups chocolate ice cream

2 cups seltzer or sparkling water
1 cup heavy cream
2 Tbsp. powdered sugar

1. Pour 2 Tbsp. chocolate syrup into each of 4 (16-oz.) glasses. Pour ½ cup milk into each glass; stir well with a long spoon or straw until blended. Spoon ½ cup ice cream into each glass; pour ½ cup seltzer into each glass, stirring until foamy.

2. In a medium bowl, beat cream and powdered sugar until soft peaks form. Top floats with whipped cream. Serve immediately.

ULTIMATE ALEXANDER

makes 5 servings   *hands-on time 5 min.*   *total time 5 min.*

¼   cup cold brewed coffee
2   pt. coffee ice cream
½   cup brandy

½   cup chocolate syrup
Garnishes: sweetened whipped cream,
    chocolate curls

1. Process cold brewed coffee, ice cream, brandy, and chocolate syrup in a blender until smooth, stopping to scrape down sides as needed. Pour into glasses. Serve immediately.

note: We tested with Häagen-Dazs Coffee Ice Cream.

Serving a frosty dessert has never been this easy. Set up a table with ingredients and let guests pick their favorite fruit-flavored soft drink to make their own colorful creations.

FIZZY FRUITY ICE CREAM FLOATS

makes 6 servings   hands-on time 5 min.   total time 5 min.

4   cups vanilla ice cream
6   (12-oz.) fruit-flavored soft drinks,
      such as grape, orange, lime, or
      black cherry

1. Place 2 (⅓-cup) scoops of vanilla ice cream into each of 6 large glasses. Pour soft drinks over ice cream. Serve immediately.

This easy holiday drink is akin to an off-the-charts milkshake. The peppermint candies add bold mint flavor as well as a kick of sweet chocolate, plus they give these frappés a festive look!

PEPPERMINT PATTY FRAPPÉS

makes 4 servings   hands-on time 10 min.   total time 10 min.

2   cups vanilla ice cream
1   cup milk
9   miniature or 3 (1.4-oz.) chocolate-covered peppermint patties, chopped

Garnishes: sweetened whipped cream, crushed peppermint candies

1. Process ice cream, milk, and chopped peppermint patties in a blender until smooth, stopping to scrape down sides as needed. Pour into glasses. Serve immediately.

note: We tested with York Peppermint Patties.

twist it up!

GROWN-UP FRAPPÉS

Decrease milk to ⅔ cup. Add ⅓ cup crème de cacao.

FROM-SCRATCH ICE CREAM
IN YOUR FAVORITE FLAVORS

HOMEMADE ICE CREAM
TIPS FOR SUCCESS

1. Be sure to use a nonreactive saucepan to cook the ice cream custard, and cook over low heat once the eggs are added. Pay close attention to the mixture and stir constantly, as to not overcook.

2. Prepare an ice bath to speed cooling the cooked custard. Cooling the custard immediately ensures that the cooking process stops, and the custard won't overcook.

3. Thoroughly chill ice-cream mixture before freezing! If you pour hot custard into the ice-cream freezer, it will melt the frozen part of the machine, and the ice cream will never freeze.

4. Be sure to layer lots of rock salt in with the ice, if using a traditional ice-cream machine with ice. It brings the temperature down faster so the ice cream freezes quickly.

5. Avoid overchurning by watching the ice cream closely. When it reaches the consistency of soft-serve ice cream, it's ready. It will become firmer in the freezer. Overchurning results in a grainy, unpleasant texture, so don't overdo it!

6. Add any stir-ins during the last minute of churning or quickly fold them into ice cream when transferring to a storage container.

BIRTHDAY CAKE ICE CREAM

makes about 1½ quarts   hands-on time 20 min.
total time 9 hours, 20 min., not including freezing

1   cup sugar
3   cups half-and-half
2   large egg yolks
2   tsp. vanilla extract
2   cups diced pound cake
     (about 4 ½ oz.)

¾   cup ready-to-spread vanilla
     frosting
¼   cup rainbow candy sprinkles

1. Whisk together first 3 ingredients in a large heavy saucepan. Cook over medium heat, whisking constantly, 8 to 10 minutes or until slightly thickened.

2. Remove from heat; pour into a bowl, and whisk in vanilla. Cool completely (about 1 hour), stirring occasionally. Place heavy-duty plastic wrap directly on warm custard (to prevent a film from forming); chill 8 to 24 hours.

3. Pour mixture into freezer container of a 1½-qt. electric ice-cream maker, and freeze according to manufacturer's instructions. (Instructions and times may vary.) After ice cream is finished churning, fold in cake, frosting, and sprinkles. Freeze in an airtight container at least 4 hours before serving.

the scoop • • • • • • •

Jump-start this recipe by purchasing a bakery pound cake from your supermarket.

This recipe packs a double popcorn flavor punch by steeping buttered popcorn in the custard and by incorporating crunchy caramel corn into the finished ice cream.

POPCORN ICE CREAM

makes 1½ quarts   hands-on time 25 min.
total time 9 hours, 55 min., not including freezing

1 ¼ cups sugar, divided
3   cups half-and-half
3   large egg yolks
5   cups buttered popped popcorn, divided

2   tsp. vanilla extract
Parchment paper
¼   cup butter
1   Tbsp. light corn syrup
¼   tsp. table salt

1. Whisk together 1 cup sugar, half-and-half, and egg yolks in a large heavy saucepan; cook over medium heat, whisking constantly, 8 to 10 minutes or until mixture slightly thickens. Remove from heat; stir in 2 cups popcorn and vanilla. Cool completely (about 1 hour), stirring occasionally. Place plastic wrap directly onto custard (to prevent a film from forming), and chill 8 to 24 hours.

2. Preheat oven to 350°. Spread remaining 3 cups popcorn onto a parchment paper-lined baking sheet. Combine remaining ¼ cup sugar, butter, corn syrup, and salt in a small saucepan; bring to a boil. Remove from heat; drizzle over popcorn, tossing to coat using a lightly greased spatula.

3. Bake at 350° for 12 minutes or until popcorn is crisp and light golden, stirring after 7 minutes. Cool completely (about 30 minutes). Break into bite-size pieces.

4. Pour custard through a wire-mesh strainer into a bowl, discarding popcorn. Pour custard into freezer container of a 1½-qt. electric ice-cream maker, and freeze according to manufacturer's instructions. (Instructions and times may vary.) After ice cream is finished churning, fold in caramel corn. Freeze in an airtight container at least 4 hours before serving.

You could describe this rich ice cream as a summer version of cream cheese frosting. Yum! Spoon a big scoop over pie or slather in between cake layers.

CREAM CHEESE ICE CREAM

makes about 1 quart   hands-on time 25 min.
total time 9 hours, 25 min., not including freezing

3   cups half-and-half
1¼ cups powdered sugar
2   large egg yolks

1   (8-oz.) package cream cheese, cubed and softened
2   tsp. vanilla bean paste or vanilla extract

1. Whisk together first 3 ingredients in a large heavy saucepan. Cook over medium heat, whisking constantly, 8 to 10 minutes or until mixture thickens slightly. Remove from heat, and whisk in cream cheese and vanilla bean paste until cheese is melted. Cool completely (about 1 hour), stirring occasionally. Place plastic wrap directly on mixture (to prevent a film from forming), and chill 8 to 24 hours.

2. Pour mixture into freezer container of a 1½-qt. electric ice-cream maker, and freeze according to manufacturer's instructions. (Instructions and times may vary.) Freeze in an airtight container 4 hours before serving.

VANILLA BEAN ICE CREAM

makes about 1 quart   hands-on time 20 min.
total time 9 hours, 20 min., not including freezing

¾ **cup sugar**	1 **cup heavy whipping cream**
2 **Tbsp. cornstarch**	1 **large egg yolk**
⅛ **tsp. table salt**	1½ **tsp. vanilla bean paste**
2 **cups milk**	

1. Whisk together first 3 ingredients in a large heavy saucepan. Gradually whisk in milk and cream. Cook over medium heat, stirring constantly, 10 to 12 minutes or until mixture thickens slightly. Remove from heat.

2. Whisk egg yolk until slightly thickened. Gradually whisk about 1 cup hot cream mixture into yolk. Add yolk mixture to remaining cream mixture, whisking constantly. Whisk in vanilla bean paste. Cool completely (about 1 hour), stirring occasionally.

3. Place plastic wrap directly on cream mixture (to prevent a film from forming), and chill 8 to 24 hours. Pour mixture into freezer container of a 1½-qt. electric ice-cream maker, and freeze according to manufacturer's instructions. (Instructions and times may vary.) Freeze in an airtight container 4 hours before serving.

the scoop • • • • • • •

Vanilla bean paste is not only what gives Vanilla Bean Ice Cream its name but it also adds intense flavor. However, you can substitute vanilla extract, if desired.

Re-create one of your ice-cream parlor favorites at home—rich chocolate ice cream with fudgy brownie bits. Top with chocolate syrup and whipped cream for a decadent sundae.

CHOCOLATE FUDGE BROWNIE ICE CREAM

makes 1½ quarts   hands-on time 35 min.
total time 10 hours, 35 min., not including freezing

1⅓ cups sugar
⅓ cup unsweetened cocoa
2½ cups half-and-half
3 large egg yolks
½ cup whipping cream

1 (4-oz.) bittersweet chocolate baking bar, chopped
1 (18.75-oz.) package chocolate supreme brownie mix
⅓ cup vegetable oil
1 large egg

1. Whisk together sugar and cocoa in a large heavy saucepan. Whisk in ½ cup half-and-half and egg yolks. Whisk in remaining 2 cups half-and-half. Cook over medium heat, whisking constantly, 8 minutes or until mixture slightly thickens. Remove from heat.

2. Microwave whipping cream and bittersweet chocolate in a medium-size microwave-safe bowl at HIGH 1 minute or until chocolate melts, whisking until smooth. Add cocoa mixture, whisking until smooth. Cool completely (about 1 hour), stirring occasionally. Place heavy-duty plastic wrap directly on warm custard (to prevent a film from forming); chill 8 to 24 hours.

3. Preheat oven to 350°. Prepare and bake brownie mix according to package directions using vegetable oil, egg, and ¼ cup water. Cool completely on a wire rack (about 1 hour).

4. Cut half of brownies into ½-inch chunks to measure 2½ cups; reserve remaining brownies for another use.

5. Pour chilled custard into freezer container of a 1½-qt. electric ice-cream maker, and freeze according to manufacturer's instructions. (Instructions and times may vary.) After ice cream is finished churning, fold in 2½ cups brownie chunks. Freeze in an airtight container at least 4 hours before serving.

189

HONEY ICE CREAM

makes 3 quarts   hands-on time 10 min.
total time 10 min., not including freezing

2   qt. half-and-half   2   Tbsp. vanilla extract
1½ cups honey

1. Stir together all ingredients, and pour into freezer container of a 1-gal. electric ice-cream maker. Freeze according to manufacturer's instructions. (Instructions and times may vary.) Freeze in an airtight container at least 1 hour before serving.

BANANAS FOSTER ICE CREAM

makes about 1 quart   hands-on time 18 min.
total time 11 hours, 12 min., not including freezing

3 cups half-and-half
1 cup firmly packed light brown sugar
3 large egg yolks
2 tsp. vanilla extract
¾ cup jarred caramel topping
2 Tbsp. dark rum
2 medium bananas, sliced

1. Whisk together first 3 ingredients in a large heavy saucepan; cook over medium heat, whisking constantly, 8 to 10 minutes or until mixture slightly thickens. Remove from heat; whisk in vanilla. Cool completely (about 1 hour), stirring occasionally. Place plastic wrap directly onto warm custard (to prevent a film from forming), and chill 8 to 24 hours.

2. Stir together caramel topping and rum in a medium saucepan; bring to a simmer over medium heat. Stir in bananas; simmer 2 minutes or until bananas are softened, stirring occasionally. Remove from heat; cool completely (about 30 minutes). Cover and chill 2 hours.

3. Pour custard into freezer container of a 1½-qt. electric ice-cream maker, and freeze according to manufacturer's instructions. (Instructions and times may vary.) After ice cream is finished churning, fold in banana mixture. Freeze in an airtight container at least 6 hours before serving.

note: We tested with Mrs. Richardson's Caramel Topping.

the scoop • • • • • • •

This recipe is best if you choose a thick, full-flavored caramel topping to mix in with the rum and bananas.

191

WHITE CHOCOLATE ICE CREAM

makes about 1 quart   hands-on time 30 min.
total time 2 hours, 40 min., not including freezing

3 (4-oz.) white chocolate baking
   bars
3 ¼ cups whole milk, divided

½ cup sugar, divided
3 large eggs
1 tsp. vanilla extract

1. Pour water to depth of 1 inch into bottom of a double boiler over medium heat; bring to a boil. Reduce heat to low, and simmer; place chocolate and ¼ cup milk in top of double boiler over simmering water. Cook, stirring occasionally, 8 to 10 minutes or until melted. Remove from heat, and cool 10 minutes.

2. Meanwhile, cook remaining 3 cups milk and ¼ cup sugar in a heavy non-aluminum saucepan over medium heat, stirring often, 8 minutes or just until it begins to steam (do not boil); remove from heat.

3. Whisk together eggs and remaining ¼ cup sugar in a large bowl. Gradually whisk 1 cup hot milk mixture into egg mixture; gradually whisk egg mixture into remaining hot milk mixture.

4. Cook over medium heat, stirring constantly, 2 to 3 minutes. (A candy thermometer should register 160° or higher.) Stir in vanilla.

5. Remove from heat, and pour mixture through a non-aluminum fine wire-mesh strainer into a bowl. Whisk in melted chocolate mixture. Cover and chill 2 hours or until cold.

6. Pour mixture into freezer container of a 1½-qt. electric ice-cream maker, and freeze according to manufacturer's instructions. (Instructions and times will vary.) Freeze in an airtight container at least 4 hours before serving.

The combination of fresh and crystallized ginger lends a unique kick of flavor to this ice cream. Pair it with fresh fruit in the summer, pumpkin pie in the fall, and all by itself in the winter.

DOUBLE GINGER ICE CREAM

makes 1½ quarts   hands-on time 20 min.
total time 9 hours, 20 min., not including freezing

3 cups half-and-half	1 (2-inch) piece fresh ginger, sliced
1 cup sugar	1 (3-oz.) package crystallized
2 large egg yolks	ginger, minced
2 tsp. vanilla extract	

1. Whisk together first 3 ingredients in a large heavy saucepan. Cook over medium heat, whisking constantly, 8 to 10 minutes or until slightly thickened. Remove from heat; whisk in vanilla and sliced fresh ginger. Cool completely (about 1 hour), stirring occasionally. Place plastic wrap directly onto warm custard (to prevent a film from forming), and chill 8 to 24 hours. Remove and discard ginger slices.

2. Pour mixture into freezer container of a 1½-qt. electric ice-cream maker, and freeze according to manufacturer's instructions. (Instructions and times may vary.) After ice cream is finished churning, fold in crystallized ginger. Freeze in an airtight container at least 4 hours before serving.

With only four ingredients you can make this super-creamy treat that tastes just like its namesake. Serve over crispy waffles or graham crackers for a fantastic dessert worth sharing.

LEMON ICEBOX PIE ICE CREAM

makes about 1 quart   hands-on time 20 min.
total time 20 min., not including freezing

3   to 4 lemons
2   cups half-and-half
1   (14-oz.) can sweetened condensed milk

¾   cup coarsely crushed graham crackers

1. Grate zest from lemons to equal 1 Tbsp. Cut lemons in half; squeeze juice from lemons into a measuring cup to equal ½ cup.

2. Whisk together half-and-half, sweetened condensed milk, and lemon juice. Pour mixture into freezer container of a 1½-qt. electric ice-cream maker, and freeze according to manufacturer's instructions. (Instructions and times may vary.) After ice cream is finished churning, stir in graham cracker crumbs and lemon zest. Freeze in an airtight container 2 hours before serving.

Bittersweet chocolate and peppermint candy combine for an irresistibly rich result. Serve this studded ice cream in chocolate-dipped waffle cones or sugar cones for a cool treat.

CHOCOLATE-PEPPERMINT ICE CREAM

makes about 1½ quarts   hands-on time 19 min.
total time 8 hours, 49 min., not including freezing

1⅓ cups sugar
⅓ cup unsweetened cocoa
2½ cups half-and-half
3 large egg yolks
½ cup whipping cream

1 (4-oz.) bittersweet chocolate baking bar, chopped
1¼ cups crushed hard peppermint candies, divided

1. Whisk together sugar and cocoa in a large heavy saucepan. Whisk in ½ cup half-and-half and egg yolks. Whisk in remaining 2 cups half-and-half. Cook over medium heat, whisking constantly, 8 to 10 minutes or until mixture slightly thickens. Remove from heat; pour into a large bowl.

2. Microwave whipping cream and chocolate in a small microwave-safe bowl at HIGH 1 to 1½ minutes or until melted and smooth, stirring at 30-second intervals. Whisk chocolate mixture into half-and-half mixture. Whisk in ¾ cup crushed peppermint candies.

3. Place plastic wrap directly onto warm custard (to prevent a film from forming), and chill 8 to 24 hours.

4. Pour mixture into freezer container of a 1½-qt. electric ice-cream maker, and freeze according to manufacturer's instructions. (Instructions and times may vary.) After ice cream is finished churning, stir in remaining ½ cup crushed peppermint candies. Freeze in an airtight container at least 6 hours before serving.

DULCE DE LECHE ICE CREAM

makes about 1½ quarts   hands-on time 14 min.
total time 8 hours, 52 min., not including freezing

2	cups whipping cream	⅛	tsp. table salt
1	cup milk	1	(14-oz.) can dulce de leche
¾	cup sugar	1	tsp. vanilla extract

1. Combine first 5 ingredients in a large heavy saucepan. Cook over medium heat, stirring constantly, 14 minutes or until dulce de leche is melted. Remove from heat; stir in vanilla. Cool completely (about 1 hour), stirring occasionally.

2. Place plastic wrap directly onto warm custard (to prevent a film from forming), and chill 8 to 24 hours.

3. Pour mixture into freezer container of a 1½-qt. electric ice-cream maker, and freeze according to manufacturer's instructions. (Instructions and times may vary.) Freeze in an airtight container at least 4 hours before serving.

Cocoa powder imparts a rich depth of flavor to this ultra-chocolatey ice cream. Add some cream-filled chocolate cookie pieces, and you've got a homemade treat worth bragging about.

CHOCOLATE MILK AND COOKIES ICE CREAM

makes about 1½ quarts   hands-on time 13 min.
total time 8 hours, 43 min., not including freezing

3   cups half-and-half
1   cup sugar
⅓   cup unsweetened cocoa
3   large egg yolks

2   tsp. vanilla extract
2   cups chopped cream-filled
    chocolate sandwich cookies
    (about 15 cookies)

1. Whisk together first 4 ingredients in a large heavy saucepan. Cook over medium heat, whisking constantly, 8 to 10 minutes or until mixture thickens slightly. Remove from heat, and whisk in vanilla. Cool completely (about 1 hour), stirring occasionally. Place heavy-duty plastic wrap directly on warm custard (to prevent a film from forming); chill 8 to 24 hours.

2. Pour mixture into freezer container of a 1½-qt. electric ice-cream maker, and freeze according to manufacturer's instructions. (Instructions and times may vary.) After ice cream is finished churning, fold in chocolate cookies: Freeze in an airtight container at least 4 hours before serving.

BLUEBERRY CHEESECAKE ICE CREAM

makes about 1 quart   hands-on time 15 min.
total time 3 hours, not including freezing

1   (8-oz.) package cream cheese, softened to room temperature
1½ cups half and half
¾   cup sugar
½   cup whole buttermilk
1½ tsp. vanilla bean paste or vanilla extract

¼   tsp. almond extract
⅛   tsp. table salt
1   cup fresh blueberries
3   Tbsp. blueberry preserves
2   tsp. lemon zest

1. Process first 7 ingredients in a blender 30 seconds or until very smooth. Cover and chill at least 2 hours or up to 2 days.

2. Pour mixture into freezer container of a 1½-qt. electric ice-cream maker, and freeze according to manufacturer's instructions. (Instructions and times may vary.)

3. Mash together blueberries, blueberry preserves, and lemon zest. After ice cream is finished churning, stir in blueberry mixture. Freeze in an airtight container 1 hour before serving or up to 1 week.

199

Avocado might seem like a weird dessert ingredient, but we promise you'll be bowled over by this super-creamy ice cream with the zing of fresh lime flavor!

AVOCADO-KEY LIME ICE CREAM

makes about 1 quart   hands-on time 15 min.
total time 3 hours, not including freezing

1   (8-oz.) package cream cheese, softened to room temperature

1½ medium-size ripe avocados, chopped

1½ cups half and half

¾   cup sugar

½   cup whole buttermilk

1   tsp. Key lime zest

¼   cup fresh Key lime juice

1½ tsp. vanilla bean paste or vanilla extract

⅛   tsp. table salt

¾   cup coarsely crumbled graham crackers

1. Process all ingredients except crumbled graham crackers in a blender 30 seconds or until very smooth. Cover and chill at least 2 hours or up to 2 days.

2. Pour mixture into freezer container of a 1½-qt. electric ice-cream maker, and freeze according to manufacturer's instructions. (Instructions and times may vary.)

3. After ice cream is finished churning, stir in coarsely crumbled graham crackers. Freeze in an airtight container 1 hour before serving or up to 1 week.

COCONUT CREAM PIE ICE CREAM

makes about 1 quart   hands-on time 20 min.
total time 9 hours, 20 min., not including freezing

¾   cup sugar
2   Tbsp. cornstarch
⅛   tsp. table salt
1   cup milk
1   cup coconut milk
1   cup heavy whipping cream

1   large egg yolk
1½   tsp. vanilla bean paste or vanilla extract
¾   cup sweetened flaked coconut, toasted

1. Whisk together first 3 ingredients in a large heavy saucepan. Gradually whisk in milk, coconut milk, and cream. Cook over medium heat, stirring constantly, 10 to 12 minutes or until mixture thickens slightly. Remove from heat.

2. Whisk egg yolk until slightly thickened. Gradually whisk about 1 cup hot cream mixture into yolk. Add yolk mixture to remaining cream mixture, whisking constantly. Whisk in vanilla bean paste. Cool 1 hour, stirring occasionally.

3. Place plastic wrap directly on cream mixture (to prevent a film from forming), and chill 8 to 24 hours.

4. Stir in toasted coconut. Pour mixture into freezer container of a 1½-qt. electric ice-cream maker, and freeze according to manufacturer's instructions. (Instructions and times may vary.) Freeze in an airtight container at least 4 hours before serving.

202

CARAMEL-CASHEW ICE CREAM

makes about 1 quart   hands-on time 10 min.
total time 6 hours, 10 min.

2 cups whipping cream
1 (14-oz.) can sweetened
   condensed milk
½ cup butterscotch-caramel
   topping

1 cup salted cashews,
   chopped
Toppings: butterscotch-caramel
   topping, chopped cashews

1. Beat whipping cream at high speed with an electric mixer until stiff peaks form.

2. Stir together sweetened condensed milk and ½ cup butterscotch-caramel topping in a large mixing bowl. Fold in whipped cream and 1 cup cashews. Freeze in an airtight container 6 to 8 hours or until firm. Serve with desired toppings.

PEACH-AND-TOASTED PECAN ICE CREAM

makes about 1 quart   hands-on time 45 min.
total time 10 hours, 45 min., not including freezing

¾ cup sugar
2 Tbsp. cornstarch
⅛ tsp. table salt
2 cups milk
1 cup heavy whipping cream
1 large egg yolk
1½ tsp. vanilla bean paste or vanilla extract

1 cup peeled and coarsely chopped peaches
2 Tbsp. light corn syrup
1½ Tbsp. butter
1 cup coarsely chopped pecans
¼ tsp. kosher salt

1. Whisk together first 3 ingredients in a large heavy saucepan. Gradually whisk in milk and whipping cream. Cook over medium heat, stirring constantly, 10 to 12 minutes or until mixture thickens slightly. Remove from heat.

2. Whisk egg yolk until slightly thickened. Gradually whisk about 1 cup hot cream mixture into yolk. Add yolk mixture to remaining cream mixture, whisking constantly. Whisk in vanilla bean paste. Cool completely (about 1 hour), stirring occasionally.

3. Meanwhile, cook peaches and corn syrup in a small saucepan over medium heat, stirring often, 4 to 5 minutes. Coarsely mash, and cool 30 minutes. Stir peach mixture into cooled cream mixture. Place plastic wrap directly on custard (to prevent a film from forming), and chill 8 to 24 hours.

4. Meanwhile, melt butter in a small skillet over medium heat; add pecans, and cook, stirring constantly, 8 to 9 minutes or until toasted and fragrant. Remove from heat, and sprinkle with ¼ tsp. kosher salt. Cool completely (about 30 minutes).

5. Pour chilled custard into freezer container of a 1½-qt. electric ice-cream maker, and freeze according to manufacturer's instructions. (Instructions and times may vary.) After ice cream is finished churning, stir in pecan mixture. Freeze in an airtight container at least 1 hour before serving.

MOCHA LATTE ICE CREAM

makes about 1 quart   hands-on time 20 min.
total time 10 hours, 5 min., not including freezing

¾ cup sugar
2 Tbsp. cornstarch
1 Tbsp. instant espresso powder
⅛ tsp. table salt
2 cups milk
1 cup heavy whipping cream
1 egg yolk

1½ tsp. vanilla bean paste or vanilla extract
1 cup chopped pecans
2 oz. finely chopped semisweet chocolate
Garnish: dark chocolate sticks

1. Whisk together first 4 ingredients in a large heavy saucepan. Gradually whisk in milk and whipping cream. Cook over medium heat, stirring constantly, 10 to 12 minutes or until mixture thickens slightly. Remove from heat.

2. Whisk egg yolk until slightly thickened. Gradually whisk about 1 cup hot cream mixture into yolk. Add yolk mixture to remaining cream mixture, whisking constantly. Whisk in vanilla bean paste. Cool 1 hour, stirring occasionally.

3. Place plastic wrap directly on custard (to prevent a film from forming), and chill 8 to 24 hours.

4. Meanwhile, preheat oven to 350°. Bake pecans in a single layer in a shallow pan 8 minutes or until toasted and fragrant, stirring once halfway through. Cool completely (about 30 minutes).

5. Pour chilled cream mixture into freezer container of a 1½-qt. electric ice-cream maker, and freeze according to manufacturer's instructions. (Instructions and times may vary.) After ice cream is finished churning, stir in pecans and chocolate. Freeze in an airtight container at least 4 hours before serving.

CHOCOLATE-RASPBERRY ICE CREAM

makes about 1 quart   hands-on time 20 min.
total time 9 hours, 20 min., not including freezing

¾   cup sugar
2   Tbsp. cornstarch
⅛   tsp. table salt
2   cups milk
1   cup heavy whipping cream
1   large egg yolk

1 ½   tsp. vanilla bean paste or vanilla extract
4   oz. finely chopped semisweet chocolate
¼   cup seedless raspberry preserves, melted

1. Whisk together first 3 ingredients in a large heavy saucepan. Gradually whisk in milk and cream. Cook over medium heat, stirring constantly, 10 to 12 minutes or until mixture thickens slightly. Remove from heat.

2. Whisk egg yolk until slightly thickened. Gradually whisk about 1 cup hot cream mixture into yolk. Add yolk mixture to remaining cream mixture, whisking constantly. Whisk in vanilla bean paste. Cool completely (about 1 hour), stirring occasionally.

3. Place plastic wrap directly on custard (to prevent a film from forming), and chill 8 to 24 hours.

4. Stir in chopped chocolate, and gently fold in melted raspberry preserves. Pour mixture into freezer container of a 1 ½-qt. electric ice-cream maker, and freeze according to manufacturer's instructions. (Instructions and times may vary.) Freeze in an airtight container until ready to serve.

Lemon zest adds bright, citrus flavor to this summer-berry ice cream. Choose juicy blackberries at the peak of season for the best results, and serve on a simple sugar cone.

BLACKBERRY-LEMON ICE CREAM

makes about 1 quart   hands-on time 13 min.
total time 8 hours, 43 min., not including freezing

3   cups half-and-half
1¼ cups sugar
3   large egg yolks
2   tsp. vanilla extract

2   cups fresh blackberries, slightly mashed
½   tsp. lemon zest

1. Whisk together first 3 ingredients in a large heavy saucepan. Cook over medium heat, whisking constantly, 8 to 10 minutes or until slightly thickened. Remove from heat; whisk in vanilla. Cool completely (about 1 hour), stirring occasionally. Place plastic wrap directly on warm custard (to prevent a film from forming); chill 8 to 24 hours.

2. Stir blackberries and lemon zest into chilled custard. Pour mixture into freezer container of a 1½-qt. electric ice-cream maker, and freeze according to manufacturer's instructions. (Instructions and times may vary.) Freeze in an airtight container at least 4 hours before serving.

BANANA-COCONUT ICE CREAM

makes about 2½ quarts   hands-on time 30 min.
total time 3 hours, 40 min., not including freezing

2 cups sweetened flaked coconut	1 (15-oz.) can cream of coconut
1 cup sugar	2 tsp. vanilla extract
6 large egg yolks	3 ripe bananas, mashed
4 cups milk	Garnish: toasted sweetened flaked
2 cups half-and-half	coconut

1. Preheat oven to 350°. Bake coconut in a shallow pan 10 minutes or until toasted, stirring occasionally.

2. Whisk together sugar, egg yolks, and milk in a heavy saucepan over medium heat; cook, whisking constantly, 20 minutes or until mixture thickens and will coat a spoon (do not boil).

3. Remove from heat; whisk in toasted coconut, half-and-half, cream of coconut, and vanilla. Fold in banana. Place plastic wrap directly on custard (to prevent a film from forming), and chill 3 hours.

4. Pour custard into freezer container of a 1-gal. electric ice-cream maker, and freeze according to manufacturer's instructions. (Instructions and times may vary.)

5. Freeze in an airtight container for at least 1 hour before serving.

PEACH-CINNAMON ICE CREAM

makes about 2½ quarts   hands-on time 20 min.
total time 4 hours, 20 min., not including freezing

4   cups peeled, diced fresh peaches
    (about 3 lb.)
1   cup peach nectar
½   cup sugar
3   large egg yolks

4   cups milk
1   cup half-and-half
1   tsp. lemon juice
½   tsp. ground cinnamon
Garnish: sliced fresh peaches

1. Combine first 3 ingredients in a medium bowl.

2. Process peach mixture, in batches, in a food processor until smooth, stopping to scrape down sides. Set aside.

3. Whisk together yolks and milk in a heavy saucepan over medium heat; cook, stirring constantly, 20 minutes or until mixture thickens and coats a spoon. Do not boil.

4. Remove from heat; whisk in peach mixture, half-and-half, lemon juice, and ground cinnamon. Place plastic wrap directly on custard (to prevent a film from forming), and chill 4 hours.

5. Pour custard into freezer container of a 6-qt. electric ice-cream maker, and freeze according to manufacturer's instructions. (Instructions and times will vary.) Freeze in an airtight container at least 4 hours before serving.

the scoop • • • • • • •

Peach nectar is a sweet, intensely flavored drink that's usually found on the international food aisle, with the fruit juices, or with the cocktail mixes.

This decadent ice cream is a great way to use summer's harvest of fresh figs. If you have any leftover, quarter them and serve them on top, along with a drizzle of honey.

CARAMELIZED FIG ICE CREAM

makes about 1½ quarts   hands-on time 1 hour, 27 min.
total time 9 hours, 57 min., not including freezing

1½ cups sugar, divided
1   lb. fresh figs, stemmed and chopped
1½ tsp. orange zest
1   Tbsp. fresh orange juice

2   Tbsp. butter
3   cups half-and-half
3   large egg yolks
2   tsp. vanilla extract

1. Combine ½ cup sugar and ¼ cup water in a large heavy saucepan; cook over medium heat 6 to 8 minutes or until sugar melts and turns a light golden brown, tipping pan to incorporate mixture. Stir in figs, zest, and juice; cook 5 to 6 minutes or until mixture is bubby and figs start to break down, stirring occasionally.

2. Remove from heat; stir in butter. Cool completely (about 1 hour). Cover and chill 8 to 24 hours.

3. Whisk together remaining 1 cup sugar, half-and-half, and egg yolks in a large heavy saucepan. Cook over medium heat, whisking constantly, 8 to 10 minutes or until mixture slightly thickens. Pour into a large bowl; whisk in vanilla. Cool completely (about 1 hour), stirring occasionally. Place plastic wrap directly onto warm custard (to prevent a film from forming), and chill 8 to 24 hours.

4. Gently stir caramelized fig mixture into half-and-half mixture. Pour mixture into freezer container of a 2-qt. electric ice-cream maker, and freeze according to manufacturer's instructions. (Instructions and times may vary.) Freeze in an airtight container at least 4 hours before serving.

PECAN CRUNCH ICE CREAM

makes about 4 quarts   hands-on time 45 min.
total time 1 hour, 45 min., not including freezing

2   cups firmly packed light brown sugar
3   cups milk
1   (12-oz.) can evaporated milk
½   tsp. table salt
4   large egg yolks

4   cups whipping cream
1   (14-oz.) can sweetened condensed milk
2   Tbsp. vanilla extract
Pecan Crunch
1   (20-oz.) bottle caramel topping

1. Stir together brown sugar and next 3 ingredients in a large saucepan over low heat, and simmer, stirring often, 1 minute. (Do not boil.)

2. Beat egg yolks until thick and lemon-colored. Gradually stir 1 cup hot brown sugar mixture into yolks. Add egg yolk mixture to remaining hot mixture; cook, stirring constantly, over low heat 2 minutes or until mixture begins to thicken. Remove pan from heat; stir in cream, condensed milk, and vanilla. Cool to room temperature (about 1 hour).

3. Pour mixture into freezer container of a 6-qt. electric ice-cream maker, and freeze according to manufacturer's instructions. (Instructions and times may vary.) After ice cream is finished churning, stir in Pecan Crunch and caramel topping. Freeze in an airtight container at least 1 hour until ready to serve.

PECAN CRUNCH

Preheat oven to 350°. Stir together ¾ cup quick-cooking oats, 1 cup chopped pecans, ¼ cup all-purpose flour, ¼ cup firmly packed light brown sugar, and ¼ cup melted butter; spread in a thin layer on a baking sheet. Bake for 15 minutes. Cool completely on a wire rack. Coarsely chop. Makes about 2 cups.

ICE CREAM SHOPPE

NO-COOK VANILLA ICE CREAM

makes 1 quart   hands-on time 15 min.
total time 45 min., not including freezing

1	(14-oz.) can sweetened condensed milk	2	Tbsp. sugar
1	(5-oz.) can evaporated milk	2	tsp. vanilla extract
		2	cups whole milk

1. Whisk all ingredients in a 2-qt. pitcher or large bowl until blended. Cover and chill 30 minutes.

2. Pour milk mixture into freezer container of a 1-qt. electric ice-cream maker, and freeze according to manufacturer's instructions. (Instructions and times may vary.)

3. Freeze in an airtight container 1 to 1½ hours before serving.

twist it up!

NO-COOK TURTLE ICE CREAM

Prepare No-Cook Vanilla Ice Cream as directed. Stir ¼ cup caramel sauce into ice cream. Remove container with ice cream from ice-cream maker, and place in freezer. Freeze 15 minutes. Microwave ½ cup semisweet chocolate morsels and 1 tsp. shortening in a microwave-safe glass bowl at HIGH 1 minute. Stir until smooth. Place ¾ cup toasted chopped pecans on a parchment paper-lined baking sheet. Drizzle pecans with melted chocolate. Freeze 5 minutes. Break into bite-size pieces. Stir chocolate-and-pecan pieces into ice cream. Place in an airtight container; freeze until firm. Makes 1½ quarts.

LIGHTENED VANILLA BEAN ICE CREAM

makes about 1 quart   hands-on time 20 min.
total time 9 hours, 20 min., not including freezing

½ cup granular sweetener for ice cream	1 cup half-and-half
2 Tbsp. cornstarch	1 large egg yolk
⅛ tsp. table salt	1½ tsp. vanilla bean paste or vanilla extract
2 cups 2% reduced-fat milk	

1. Whisk together first 3 ingredients in a large heavy saucepan. Gradually whisk in milk and half-and-half. Cook over medium heat, stirring constantly, 8 to 10 minutes or until mixture thickens slightly. Remove from heat.

2. Whisk egg yolk until slightly thickened. Gradually whisk about 1 cup hot cream mixture into yolk. Add yolk mixture to remaining cream mixture, whisking constantly. Whisk in vanilla bean paste.

3. Pour mixture through a fine wire-mesh strainer into a bowl, discarding solids. Cool 1 hour, stirring occasionally. Place plastic wrap directly on custard (to prevent a film from forming); chill 8 to 24 hours.

4. Pour custard into freezer container of a 1½-qt. electric ice-cream maker, and freeze according to manufacturer's instructions. (Instructions and times may vary.) Freeze in an airtight container 1 to 1½ hours before serving.

note: We tested with Whey Low 100% All Natural Granular Sweetener for Ice Cream. Granulated sugar may be substituted.

twist it up!

CHERRY-BOURBON ICE CREAM

Stir in ½ cup drained and coursely chopped canned, pitted cherries in heavy syrup and 3 Tbsp. bourbon halfway through freezing.

COFFEE-CHOCOLATE ICE CREAM

Substitute 2 Tbsp. instant espresso for 1½ tsp. vanilla bean paste. Stir in ¼ cup shaved semisweet chocolate baking bar halfway through freezing.

KEY LIME PIE ICE CREAM

Omit vanilla bean paste. Stir in 1 tsp. Key lime zest, ⅓ cup Key lime juice, and ½ cup coarsely crushed graham crackers halfway through freezing.

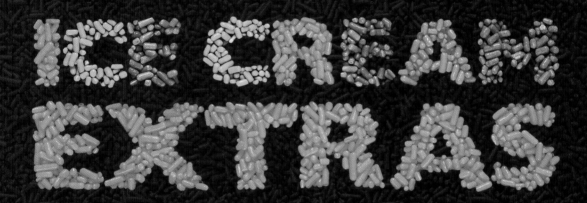

ICE CREAM
EXTRAS

TOPPINGS, SAUCES, CRUSTS, AND COOKIES

Bacon-Praline Crumble

BACON-PRALINE CRUMBLE

makes 7½ cups   hands-on time 21 min.   total time 36 min.

Parchment paper
1   Tbsp. butter, softened
3   cups firmly packed light brown
     sugar
1   cup whipping cream
¼   cup butter

2   Tbsp. light corn syrup
1   cup crushed mini-pretzel twists
1   cup cooked and crumbled bacon
     slices (about 12 slices)
1   tsp. vanilla extract

1. Line a jelly-roll pan with parchment paper; grease paper heavily with butter. Combine brown sugar and next 3 ingredients in a heavy Dutch oven; bring to a boil over medium heat, stirring constantly. Boil, stirring occasionally, 10 to 12 minutes or until a candy thermometer registers 236° (soft ball stage).

2. Remove from heat; immediately stir in pretzels, bacon, and vanilla using a wooden spoon. Stir constantly 1 to 2 minutes or just until mixture begins to lose its gloss. Quickly pour into prepared pan, spreading to ¼-inch thickness. Let stand 10 to 15 minutes or until cool and firm. Break into bite-size pieces.

GINGER-CASHEW CRUNCH

makes 3¾ cups   hands-on time 20 min.   total time 35 min.

¾   cup firmly packed light brown
     sugar
3   Tbsp. butter

1   tsp. kosher salt
1½   tsp. grated fresh ginger
2   cups unsalted cashews

1. Cook sugar in a 10-inch nonstick skillet over medium-high heat 3 minutes or until melted, stirring constantly. Stir in butter, salt, and ginger; cook, stirring constantly, 1 minute or until butter is melted and mixture is smooth. Stir in cashews; cook, stirring constantly, 1 minute or until nuts are fully coated and sugar caramelizes.

2. Quickly pour mixture onto a lightly greased baking sheet, separating nuts with 2 forks. Cool on pan on a wire rack 15 minutes. Break mixture into bite-size pieces.

CHOCOLATE-PECAN PIE GRANOLA

makes 6 cups   hands-on time 10 min.   total time 1 hour, 5 min.

½   cup butter, melted
½   cup dark corn syrup
¼   cup firmly packed light brown sugar
1   tsp. vanilla extract
⅛   tsp. table salt

3   cups uncooked regular oats
1½   cups coarsely chopped pecans
½   cup toasted wheat germ
4   oz. semisweet chocolate baking bars, chopped

1. Preheat oven to 325°. Stir together first 5 ingredients in a large bowl. Add oats, pecans, and wheat germ, stirring to coat. Spread mixture in a lightly greased 15- x 10-inch jelly-roll pan.

2. Bake at 325° for 25 to 30 minutes or until toasted, stirring every 10 minutes. Cool completely in pan on a wire rack (about 30 minutes). Stir in chocolate. Store in an airtight container at room temperature up to 3 days, or freeze up to 6 months.

BALSAMIC STRAWBERRIES

makes 8 servings   *hands-on time 5 min.*   *total time 1 hour, 5 min.*

2   cups sliced fresh strawberries   4   tsp. balsamic vinegar
¼   cup sugar

1. Stir together sliced strawberries, sugar, and balsamic vinegar; let stand 1 hour.

TROPICAL FRUIT TOPPING

makes 3 cups   *hands-on time 10 min.*   *total time 1 hour, 10 min.*

1   small papaya   1   (12-oz.) jar apricot preserves
1   mango   1   Tbsp. rum
2   kiwifruit   1   cup pineapple tidbits

1. Peel and cut papaya, mango, and kiwifruit into small chunks.

2. Stir together apricot preserves and 1 Tbsp. rum in a large bowl; add papaya, mango, kiwifruit, and pineapple, tossing to coat. Cover and chill 1 hour. Serve with a slotted spoon.

WARM BLACKBERRY SAUCE

makes 6 servings   hands-on time 10 min.   total time 10 min.

2	pt. fresh blackberries, halved	2½	tsp. grated orange zest
¼	cup sugar	½	tsp. ground ginger

1. Stir together all ingredients in a saucepan over medium heat; cook, stirring constantly, 5 minutes or until thoroughly heated. Serve warm, or cool to room temperature before serving.

FRESH STRAWBERRY SYRUP

makes about 2 cups   hands-on time 10 min.   total time 10 min.

1	qt. fresh strawberries, sliced	¼	cup orange liqueur or orange juice
½	cup sugar	1	tsp. grated orange zest

1. Combine all ingredients in a saucepan, and let stand 30 minutes or until sugar dissolves. Cook over low heat, stirring occasionally, 5 minutes or until warm. Store in an airtight container in the refrigerator.

Caramel Apple Topping

CARAMEL APPLE TOPPING

makes about 4 cups   hands-on time 25 min.   total time 45 min.

¼   cup butter
½   cup sugar
1   tsp. fresh lemon juice

5   large Granny Smith apples (about
    2½ lb.), peeled and cut into
    ½-inch-thick wedges

1. Melt butter in a large skillet over medium heat; add sugar and lemon juice, and cook, stirring constantly with a long-handled wooden spoon, 5 to 6 minutes or until mixture turns a light golden brown.

2. Add apple wedges. Cook, stirring often, 15 to 18 more minutes or until apples are tender and caramelized. Remove from heat; cool 20 minutes.

CARAMEL SAUCE

makes about 1½ cups   hands-on time 10 min.   total time 25 min.

1   cup firmly packed light brown
    sugar
½   cup butter

¼   cup whipping cream
¼   cup honey

1. Bring brown sugar, butter, whipping cream, and honey to a boil in a medium saucepan over medium-high heat, stirring constantly; boil, stirring constantly, 2 minutes. Remove from heat, and cool 15 minutes before serving.

2. Store in an airtight container in refrigerator up to 1 week.

SALTED BOURBON-SPIKED TOFFEE SAUCE

makes 1²/₃ cups   hands-on time 15 min.   total time 45 min.

1 cup firmly packed light brown sugar	2 Tbsp. light corn syrup
¾ cup unsalted butter	¼ cup bourbon or whiskey, divided
1 cup heavy cream	½ tsp. sea salt
	1 tsp. vanilla extract

1. Bring sugar, butter, cream, corn syrup, 2 Tbsp. bourbon, and salt to a boil in a medium-size heavy saucepan over medium heat. Boil, whisking often, 8 to 10 minutes or until sugar dissolves and mixture is slightly thickened. Remove from heat.

2. Cool completely (about 30 minutes). Stir in remaining 2 Tbsp. bourbon and vanilla.

the scoop • • • • • • •

This toffee sauce is so addictive it's doubtful storage will be an issue; however, toffee sauce will keep stored in the refrig-erator for up to 1 month.

HOT FUDGE ICE CREAM TOPPING

makes 1½ cups   hands-on time 15 min.   total time 15 min.

2   (1-oz.) semisweet chocolate
   squares
¾   cup sugar
1   cup evaporated milk

2   Tbsp. butter
1   tsp. vanilla extract
1   Tbsp. bourbon (optional)

1. Melt chocolate in a heavy saucepan over low heat. Stir in sugar until smooth. Gradually add milk, stirring until smooth. Bring to a boil over medium heat, stirring constantly. Boil, stirring constantly, 6 minutes. Remove from heat, and stir in butter, vanilla, and bourbon, if desired. Store in refrigerator up to 3 weeks.

MAPLE-PECAN ICE CREAM TOPPING

makes 1 cup   hands-on time 15 min.   total time 25 min.

¾   cup firmly packed light brown
   sugar
3   Tbsp. maple syrup

2   Tbsp. butter
½   cup chopped toasted pecans
¼   cup whipping cream

1. Cook brown sugar, maple syrup, and ¼ cup water in a saucepan over medium heat, stirring constantly, 6 to 8 minutes or until a candy thermometer registers 234° (soft ball stage). Remove from heat; stir in butter. Cool 10 minutes.

2. Stir in pecans and whipping cream. Store in refrigerator up to 3 weeks. Serve warm over ice cream.

PEANUT BUTTER-HOT CHOCOLATE SAUCE

makes 2 cups   hands-on time 10 min.   total time 10 min.

1   cup heavy cream
⅓   cup sugar
1½ (4-oz.) bittersweet chocolate
    baking bars, chopped

½   cup creamy peanut butter
1   Tbsp. Asian Sriracha hot
    chili sauce

1. Combine heavy cream and sugar in a small saucepan; cook over medium heat, stirring constantly, 3 minutes or until sugar dissolves.
2. Remove from heat. Add chocolate, stirring until chocolate is melted. Stir in peanut butter and Sriracha. Serve warm over ice cream. Store in refrigerator.

PEANUT BUTTER SAUCE

makes 2½ cups   hands-on time 10 min.   total time 10 min.

1⅓ cups miniature marshmallows
1   (14-oz.) can sweetened
    condensed milk

1   cup chunky peanut butter
⅓   cup light corn syrup

1. Melt marshmallows and sweetened condensed milk in a small saucepan over medium heat, stirring constantly. Add peanut butter and corn syrup, stirring until blended. Store sauce in the refrigerator up to 1 month, and reheat before serving.

CHERRY SAUCE

makes 1⅓ cups   hands-on time 15 min.   total time 1 hour, 15 min.

- 2 (12-oz.) packages frozen cherries
- ⅓ cup sugar
- ⅓ cup cold water
- 2 tsp. cornstarch
- 2 Tbsp. Kirsch or brandy
- ½ tsp. vanilla extract
- Pinch of table salt

1. Stir together cherries, sugar, cold water, and cornstarch in a medium saucepan. Cook over medium-low heat, stirring often, 12 to 15 minutes or until thickened. Remove from heat, and stir in Kirsch or brandy, vanilla, and salt. Cool completely (about 1 hour).

HONEY-PECAN BUTTERSCOTCH SAUCE

makes 1½ cups   hands-on time 10 min.   total time 40 min.

- 1 cup firmly packed light brown sugar
- ½ cup butter
- ¼ cup milk
- ¼ cup honey
- ¾ cup coarsely chopped toasted pecans

1. Bring brown sugar, butter, milk, and honey to a boil in a medium saucepan over medium-high heat, stirring constantly; boil, stirring constantly, 2 minutes. Remove from heat, and cool 30 minutes. Stir in pecans.

Cherry Sauce

ALL-TIME FAVORITE CHOCOLATE CHIP COOKIES

makes about 5 dozen cookies   hands-on time 30 min.   total time 1 hour, 5 min.

¾ cup butter, softened
¾ cup granulated sugar
¾ cup firmly packed dark brown sugar
2 large eggs
1½ tsp. vanilla extract
2¼ cups plus 2 Tbsp. all-purpose flour

1 tsp. baking soda
¾ tsp. table salt
1½ (12-oz.) packages semisweet chocolate morsels
Parchment paper

1. Preheat oven to 350°. Beat butter and sugars at medium speed with a heavy-duty electric mixer until creamy. Add eggs and vanilla, beating until blended.

2. Combine flour, baking soda, and salt in a small bowl; gradually add to butter mixture, beating just until blended. Beat in morsels just until combined. Drop by tablespoonfuls onto parchment paper-lined baking sheets.

3. Bake at 350° for 10 to 14 minutes or until desired degree of doneness. Remove to wire racks, and cool completely (about 15 minutes).

CHEWY CHOCOLATE COOKIES

makes about 5 dozen   hands-on time 20 min.   total time 50 min.

1¼ cups butter, softened
2   cups sugar
2   large eggs
2   tsp. vanilla extract
2   cups all-purpose flour

¾   cup cocoa
1   tsp. baking soda
½   tsp. table salt
1   cup chopped pecans

1. Preheat oven to 350°. Beat butter at medium speed with an electric mixer until creamy; gradually add sugar, beating well. Add eggs and vanilla, beating until well blended.

2. Combine flour and next 3 ingredients; gradually add to butter mixture, beating at low speed until blended after each addition. Stir in pecans. Shape dough into 1½-inch balls, and place on lightly greased baking sheets.

3. Bake at 350° for 18 to 20 minutes or until lightly browned. Cool in pan 1 minute; remove to wire racks to cool completely.

the scoop . . . .

Turn these oversize cookies into ice-cream sandwiches by spreading ¼ cup vanilla ice cream between them. Wrap sandwiches individually, and freeze until firm.

FLOURLESS PEANUT BUTTER-CHOCOLATE CHIP COOKIES

makes 2 dozen   hands-on time 30 min.   total time 1 hour, 14 min.

1   cup creamy peanut butter
¾   cup sugar
1   large egg
½   tsp. baking soda
¼   tsp. table salt
1   cup semisweet chocolate morsels
Parchment paper

1. Preheat oven to 350°. Stir together peanut butter and next 4 ingredients in a medium bowl until well blended. Stir in chocolate morsels.

2. Drop dough by rounded tablespoonfuls 2 inches apart onto parchment paper-lined baking sheets.

3. Bake at 350° for 12 to 14 minutes or until puffed and lightly browned. Cool on baking sheets on a wire rack 5 minutes. Transfer to wire rack, and cool 15 minutes.

Shortbread serves as a base for this chocolatey pecan toffee. These cookies make excellent food gifts, but make extra because it'll be hard to give this sweet treat away.

PECAN-TOFFEE SHORTBREAD

makes 2 dozen   hands-on time 30 min.   total time 2 hours

1   cup butter, softened
⅔   cup firmly packed light brown
    sugar
⅓   cup cornstarch
2   cups all-purpose flour
¼   tsp. table salt

2   tsp. vanilla extract
2   cups coarsely chopped toasted
    pecans, divided
1   (12-oz.) package semisweet
    chocolate morsels

1. Preheat oven to 350°. Beat butter at medium speed with an electric mixer until creamy. Stir together brown sugar and cornstarch; gradually add to butter, beating at low speed until well blended. Stir together flour and salt; gradually add flour mixture to butter mixture, beating at low speed just until blended. Add vanilla and 1 cup pecans, beating at low speed just until blended.

2. Turn dough out onto a lightly greased baking sheet; pat or roll dough into an 11- x 14-inch rectangle, leaving at least a 1-inch border on all sides of baking sheet.

3. Bake at 350° for 20 minutes or until golden brown. Remove from baking sheet to a wire rack; sprinkle shortbread with chocolate morsels. Let stand 5 minutes; gently spread melted morsels over shortbread. Sprinkle with remaining 1 cup pecans, and cool completely (about 1 hour). Cut or break shortbread into 2- to 3-inch pieces.

Rich chocolate and ooey-gooey marshmallows give these cookies their savory sweetness. Serve them alongside a bowl of ice cream, or turn them into ice-cream sandwiches with chocolate ice cream.

MISSISSIPPI MUD COOKIES

makes 3 dozen   hands-on time 25 min.   total time 35 min.

1 cup semisweet chocolate morsels	½ tsp. table salt
½ cup butter, softened	1 cup chopped pecans
1 cup sugar	½ cup milk chocolate morsels
2 large eggs	Parchment paper
1 tsp. vanilla extract	1 cup plus 2 Tbsp. miniature
1½ cups all-purpose flour	marshmallows
1 tsp. baking powder	

1. Preheat oven to 350°. Microwave semisweet chocolate morsels in a small microwave-safe glass bowl at HIGH 1 minute or until smooth, stirring at 30-second intervals.

2. Beat butter and sugar at medium speed with an electric mixer until creamy; add eggs, 1 at a time, beating until blended after each addition. Beat in vanilla and melted chocolate.

3. Combine flour, baking powder, and salt; gradually add to chocolate mixture, beating until well blended. Stir in chopped pecans and ½ cup milk chocolate morsels.

4. Drop dough by heaping tablespoonfuls onto parchment paper-lined baking sheets. Press 3 marshmallows into each portion of dough.

5. Bake at 350° for 10 to 12 minutes or until set. Remove to wire racks.

These chocolate-drizzled, salty-sweet cookie sticks are the perfect accompaniment to a simple bowl of vanilla or chocolate ice cream, and are ideal for a party!

PRETZEL-TOFFEE-CHOCOLATE CHIP COOKIE STICKS

makes 16 servings   hands-on time 12 min.
total time 1 hour, 30 min.

1   (17.5-oz.) package chocolate chip cookie mix
½   cup butter, softened
1   large egg
1   cup mini-pretzel twists, coarsely crushed

¾   cup toffee bits
Parchment paper
1   (4-oz.) semisweet chocolate baking bar, chopped

1. Preheat oven to 350°. Stir together first 3 ingredients in a medium bowl until well blended. Stir in crushed pretzels and toffee bits. Press dough into a 12- x 10-inch rectangle on a parchment paper-lined baking sheet. Make ¼-inch-deep cuts in top of dough with a sharp knife to form 16 (5- x 1½-inch) cookie sticks.

2. Bake at 350° for 15 to 20 minutes or until golden brown. Immediately cut cookie along score lines; wipe knife clean between cuts. Cool completely on baking sheet (about 30 minutes).

3. Microwave chocolate in a small microwave-safe bowl at HIGH 1 minute or until melted and smooth, stirring at 30-second intervals. Drizzle cookie sticks with chocolate. Chill 30 minutes or until chocolate is set.

CHOCOLATE-CREAM COOKIE CRUST

makes 1 (9-inch) piecrust   hands-on time 5 min.   total time 45 min.

18   cream-filled chocolate or vanilla   3   Tbsp. butter, melted
       sandwich cookies, broken

1. Preheat oven to 350°. Process cookie pieces in a food processor until finely ground. With processor running, pour butter through food chute; pulse 4 or 5 times, just until blended.

2. Firmly press crumb mixture into bottom and up sides of a 9-inch pie plate. Bake at 350° for 10 minutes. Remove from oven to a wire rack, and cool completely (about 30 minutes).

VANILLA WAFER CRUST

makes 1 (9-inch) piecrust   hands-on time 8 min.
total time 1 hour, 18 min.

62 vanilla wafers, finely crushed
    (about 2 cups)
6   Tbsp. butter, melted

2   Tbsp. sugar
⅛   tsp. table salt

1. Preheat oven to 350°. Stir together all ingredients; firmly press mixture on bottom and up sides of a 9-inch pie plate or a 9-inch deep-dish pie plate.

2. Bake at 350° for 10 to 12 minutes or until golden brown. Remove from oven, and cool completely (about 1 hour).

NO-BAKE CHOCOLATE WAFER CRUST

Makes 1 (9-inch) piecrust   hands-on time 8 min.   total time 38 min.

1   (9-oz.) package chocolate wafer
    cookies

½   cup butter, melted

1. Process wafers in a food processor until finely ground. Stir together wafer crumbs and butter. Firmly press mixture on bottom and up sides of a lightly greased 9-inch pie plate.
2. Freeze 30 minutes or until set.

BUTTERY COOKIE CRUST

makes 1 (9-inch) piecrust   hands-on time 10 min.   total time 40 min.

1   (8.8-oz.) package crisp, gourmet cookies   ⅓   cup butter, melted

1. Process cookies in a food processor until finely ground. Stir together crumbs and melted butter. Press on bottom and up sides of a lightly greased 9-inch pie plate. Freeze 30 minutes or until set.

note: We tested with Lotus Biscoff Cookies.

GRAHAM CRACKER CRUST

makes 1 (9-inch) piecrust   hands-on time 10 min.   total time 50 min.

1½ cups graham cracker crumbs   3   Tbsp. sugar
6   Tbsp. butter, melted

1. Preheat oven to 350°. Stir together all ingredients in a medium bowl. Press crumb mixture on bottom and up sides of a 9-inch pie plate or a 9-inch deep-dish pie plate.

2. Bake at 350° for 10 to 12 minutes or until lightly browned. Remove from oven to a wire rack, and cool completely (about 30 minutes).

PRETZEL CRUST

makes 1 (9-inch) piecrust   hands-on time 10 min.   total time 40 min.

4   cups pretzel twists   2   Tbsp. sugar
½   cup butter, melted

1. Preheat oven to 350°. Process all ingredients in a food processor until pretzels are finely ground. Firmly press mixture onto bottom of a lightly greased 10-inch springform pan.

2. Bake at 350° for 10 minutes. Cool completely in pan on a wire rack.

Buttery Cookie Crust

DIPPED-AND-SPRINKLED WAFFLE CONES AND BOWLS

makes 6 servings   hands-on time 27 min.   total time 1 hour, 12 min.

½	cup sugar	1	large egg white
2	Tbsp. butter, melted	⅔	cup all-purpose flour
½	tsp. vanilla extract	1½	cups chopped almonds or 1 cup rainbow candy sprinkles
¼	tsp. table salt		
1	large egg	8	oz. semisweet chocolate, chopped

1. Preheat waffle iron to medium setting. Whisk together first 6 ingredients in a medium bowl until blended. Whisk in flour until blended.

2. Spoon about 3 Tbsp. batter onto center of preheated waffle iron; close lid, and cook 2 minutes or until golden brown. Remove waffle, and, if making cones, immediately place around rolling cone to form a cone shape. If making bowls, immediately place over an inverted 6-oz. custard cup or small glass bowl. Cool on rolling cone or custard cup (about 1 minute). Transfer waffle cone or bowl to a wire rack. Repeat procedure with remaining batter.

3. Place almonds or sprinkles in a shallow dish or pie plate. Microwave chocolate in a medium-size, microwave-safe bowl at HIGH 1 minute or until melted, stirring at 30-second intervals. Holding waffle cone or bowl upside down, dip edges in melted chocolate. Immediately dip chocolate-coated edges in almonds or sprinkles. Place coated cones or bowls on wax paper until chocolate is set (about 45 minutes).

the scoop · · · · · · ·

To hold cones upright while chocolate sets, cut the bottoms out of 6 large foam drinking cups. Place cups upside-down on work surface; place dipped cones into holes in bottom of cups.

METRIC EQUIVALENTS

The recipes that appear in this cookbook use the standard U.S. method for measuring liquid and dry or solid ingredients (teaspoons, tablespoons, and cups). The information on this chart is provided to help cooks outside the United States successfully use these recipes. All equivalents are approximate.

Metric Equivalents for Different Types of Ingredients

A standard cup measure of a dry or solid ingredient will vary in weight depending on the type of ingredient. A standard cup of liquid is the same volume for any type of liquid. Use the following chart when converting standard cup measures to grams (weight) or milliliters (volume).

Standard Cup	Fine Powder (ex. flour)	Grain (ex. rice)	Granular (ex. sugar)	Liquid Solids (ex. butter)	Liquid (ex. milk)
1	140 g	150 g	190 g	200 g	240 ml
¾	105 g	113 g	143 g	150 g	180 ml
⅔	93 g	100 g	125 g	133 g	160 ml
½	70 g	75 g	95 g	100 g	120 ml
⅓	47 g	50 g	63 g	67 g	80 ml
¼	35 g	38 g	48 g	50 g	60 ml
⅛	18 g	19 g	24 g	25 g	30 ml

Useful Equivalents for Liquid Ingredients by Volume

¼ tsp				=	1 ml
½ tsp				=	2 ml
1 tsp				=	5 ml
3 tsp	=	1 Tbsp	= ½ fl oz	=	15 ml
		2 Tbsp	= ⅛ cup = 1 fl oz	=	30 ml
		4 Tbsp	= ¼ cup = 2 fl oz	=	60 ml
		5⅓ Tbsp	= ⅓ cup = 3 fl oz	=	80 ml
		8 Tbsp	= ½ cup = 4 fl oz	=	120 ml
		10⅔ Tbsp	= ⅔ cup = 5 fl oz	=	160 ml
		12 Tbsp	= ¾ cup = 6 fl oz	=	180 ml
		16 Tbsp	= 1 cup = 8 fl oz	=	240 ml
		1 pt	= 2 cups = 16 fl oz	=	480 ml
		1 qt	= 4 cups = 32 fl oz	=	960 ml
			33 fl oz	=	1000 ml = 1 l

Useful Equivalents for Dry Ingredients by Weight

(To convert ounces to grams, multiply the number of ounces by 30.)

1 oz	=	1/16 lb	=	30 g
4 oz	=	¼ lb	=	120 g
8 oz	=	½ lb	=	240 g
12 oz	=	¾ lb	=	360 g
16 oz	=	1 lb	=	480 g

Useful Equivalents for Length

(To convert inches to centimeters, multiply the number of inches by 2.5.)

1 in			=	2.5 cm	
6 in	= ½ ft		=	15 cm	
12 in	= 1 ft		=	30 cm	
36 in	= 3 ft	= 1 yd	=	90 cm	
40 in			=	100 cm	= 1 m

Useful Equivalents for Cooking/Oven Temperatures

	Fahrenheit	Celsius	Gas Mark
Freeze water	32° F	0° C	
Room temperature	68° F	20° C	
Boil water	212° F	100° C	
Bake	325° F	160° C	3
	350° F	180° C	4
	375° F	190° C	5
	400° F	200° C	6
	425° F	220° C	7
	450° F	230° C	8
Broil			Grill

INDEX

ISBN-13: 978-0-8487-4295-9
ISBN-10: 0-8487-4295-8
Library of Congress Control Number: 2013955774

Printed in the United States of America
First Printing 2014

Oxmoor House

Vice President, Brand Publishing: Laura Sappington
Editorial Director: Leah McLaughlin
Creative Director: Felicity Keane
Senior Brand Manager: Daniel Fagan
Senior Editor: Rebecca Brennan
Managing Editor: Elizabeth Tyler Austin
Assistant Managing Editor: Jeanne de Lathouder

Scooped
Editor: Allison E. Cox
Art Director: Christopher Rhoads
Senior Designer: Melissa Clark
Executive Food Director: Grace Parisi
Assistant Test Kitchen Manager: Alyson Moreland Haynes
Recipe Developers and Testers: Wendy Ball, R.D.;
    Tamara Goldis, R.D.; Stefanie Maloney; Callie Nash;
    Karen Rankin; Leah Van Deren
Food Stylists: Victoria E. Cox, Margaret Monroe Dickey,
    Catherine Crowell Steele
Photography Director: Jim Bathie
Senior Photographer: Hélène Dujardin
Senior Photo Stylist: Kay E. Clarke
Photo Stylist: Mindi Shapiro Levine
Assistant Photo Stylist:
    Mary Louise Menendez
Senior Production Manager:
    Sue Chodakiewicz
Assistant Production Manager:
    Diane Rose Keener

Contributors
Project Editor: Melissa Brown
Compositor: Frances Higginbotham
Recipe Developers and Testers: Caroline M. Wright,
    Jan Smith
Copy Editors: Rebecca Benton, Adrienne Davis
Indexer: Nanette Cardon
Fellows: Ali Carruba, Elizabeth Laseter, Amy Pinney,
    Madison Taylor Pozzo, Deanna Sakal, April Smitherman,
    Megan Thompson, Tonya West
Food Stylists: Erica Hopper, William Smith

Southern Living®
Editor: M. Lindsay Bierman
Creative Director: Robert Perino
Managing Editor: Candace Higginbotham
Executive Editors: Hunter Lewis, Jessica S. Thuston
Deputy Food Director: Whitney Wright
Test Kitchen Director: Robby Melvin
Associate Food Editor: Norman King
Test Kitchen Specialist/Food Styling:
    Vanessa McNeil Rocchio
Test Kitchen Professionals: Pam Lolley, Angela Sellers
Recipe Editor: JoAnn Weatherly
Copy Editor: Ashley Leath
Style Director: Heather Chadduck Hillegas
Director of Photography: Jeanne Dozier Clayton
Photographers: Robbie Caponetto, Laurey W. Glenn,
    Hector Sanchez
Assistant Photo Editor: Kate Phillips Robertson
Photo Coordinator: Chris Ellenbogen
Senior Photo Stylist: Buffy Hargett
Assistant Photo Stylist: Caroline Murphy Cunningham
Photo Administrative Assistant: Courtney Authement
Editorial Assistant: Pat York

Time Home Entertainment Inc.

Publisher: Jim Childs
Vice President, Brand & Digital Strategy: Steven Sandonato
Vice President, Finance: Vandana Patel
Executive Director, Marketing Services: Carol Pittard
Executive Director, Retail & Special Sales: Tom Mifsud
Executive Publishing Director: Joy Butts
Publishing Director: Megan Pearlman
Director, Bookazine Development & Marketing:
    Laura Adam
Associate General Counsel:
    Helen Wan